Also by Daniel Rhodes

Clay and Glazes for the Potter, revised edition
    Chilton Book Company

Kilns: Design, Construction and Operation
    Chilton Book Company

Stoneware and Porcelain: The Art of High-Fired Pottery
    Chilton Book Company

Tamba Pottery: The Timeless Art of a Japanese Village
    Kodansha International, Ltd.

POTTERY FORM

DANIEL RHODES

PHOTOGRAPHS BY
THOMAS LIDEN

CHILTON BOOK COMPANY
RADNOR, PENNSYLVANIA

Manufactured in the United States of America
Designed by Cypher Associates

Library of Congress Cataloging in Publication Data

Rhodes, Daniel, 1911–
    Pottery form.

    (Chilton's creative crafts series)
    Includes index.
    1. Pottery craft.   I. Title.
TT290.R47   1976   738.1   76-301
ISBN 0-8019-5935-7

1 2 3 4 5 6 7 8 9 0   5 4 3 2 1 0 9 8 7 6

FOR LILAMANI

CONTENTS

PREFACE

This book is concerned with pottery forms. Along with my previously published books *Clay and Glazes for the Potter* and *Kilns* (both published by Chilton Book Company), it completes a trilogy. It actually could be considered the first and basic book of the trilogy because pottery begins with forming. The study, formulation, and firing of various clay bodies and glazes would be meaningless without pots which are worth glazing and firing. I began this book many years ago but abandoned it when I realized that the state of my knowledge and skills had not reached a point which gave me sufficient assurance to write about a subject which was very much central to my concerns. I still feel myself to be a student of pottery, but my trepidation at approaching this task is tempered by the knowledge that it is "now or never." Many of the viewpoints expressed here have become clear to me only recently.

In writing this book I have had in mind those who wish to enlarge and deepen their understanding of pottery-making and to become better acquainted with the meanings and traditions of form in pottery. My interest has been in the way technique affects form and in the forms as they evolved to fulfill function. Techniques of forming, such as throwing, modeling, and coiling give to pottery its particular substance, feel, tactility, and energy. The function of pots has given rise to their structure, to the arrangement and relationship of parts. Pottery is both felt as a form and experienced as an adjunct to life through use. I have organized the book around these two themes. The potter and ceramist, no matter at what level he is working or in what vein he is seeking his gold, needs to acquaint himself with the forms which the craft has evolved. He needs to experience personally a variety of techniques and to know something about the origins and contexts of the various forms. To actually learn to make pots well requires extended study, preferably with a teacher, and the information given here on how to do certain things is not intended to be a complete technical guide. A growing number of books offer information of this kind, but attention to the actual quality of pots as distinct from instructions on how to make pots has generally been lacking.

Pottery Form

Since my book deals principally with traditional forms, it may be thought that there is an implied undervaluing of the new emerging culture as expressed in creative form. But in pottery (and this book is about pottery, not about sculpture in clay) it makes much sense to consider the known forms which have been worked out and handed down to us by our ancestors as a starting point, a kind of base camp from which we can push off into unfamiliar territory. Students who are knowledgeable about the traditions of their craft have an advantage. In the arts and crafts, ignorance can only hinder one from finding that secure stance from which one can work with bedrock honesty.

Pottery, one of the oldest and most widely practiced of the crafts, is a venerable tradition intimately entwined with man's daily life, with his aspirations and dreams, with his playfulness, and with his need to seek symbols and signs for the forces surrounding him. Pottery allows man's unselfconscious shaping of his own image in the clay. This tradition, always changing and taking on new meaning, is alive today in the work of countless pottery makers, some still working with age-old methods in "underdeveloped" countries, some seeking personal expression and release from the conditions of modern life, some working as professionals earning their livelihood in an ancient and honorable craft. The tradition also exists and is kept alive by the challenge of many contemporary clay workers who have sought new forms, new visions, new ways of working and who have made us see pottery with vividness even in parodies which mock it. I have not included here any discussion of sculptural forms or of the myriad and often hard to name expressive objects being made out of clay which are not pottery. These are outside the scope of the book, and I hope the omission will not be taken as some sort of prejudice on my part in favor of pottery as against other creative forms in clay.

I have excluded the topic of molds and pottery made from molds because the mold is a means to reproduce form in multiples. Thus, it is an industrial tool rather than a method of forming which has any implications, other than restrictive, for the form itself. I can think of no clay form made in a mold which could not be made by hand.

All of the illustrations are of my own work, and most of the pieces illustrated were made primarily for this book. I have been forced by the nature of the study to take on the job of making pieces to illustrate a wide variety of pottery forms. I decided not to draw on the vast storehouses of past and present accomplishments because examples from the past and finished work by contemporary potters are, in the present context, either too personal and individuated, or too specifically evocative of certain places, cultures, and times. I wanted to show the basic elements of form, without any involvement of glaze, color, or decoration. There was no way to do this except to prepare the examples myself. I hope to be spared any comparison between the examples shown here and masterworks of the past or present. They are *illustrations* of points made in the text.

Most of the pictures were taken of the wet or leatherhard piece, before drying or bisquing had taken away the freshness of damp clay. I have included a few fired and glazed pieces which serve to illustrate the considerable change which can occur to the piece as it is actually finished in the fire. Surface, although outside the present discussion, is just as much a part of pottery as is form. The drawings illustrate points which I thought might be more clearly shown by this method. The photographs of living forms speak for themselves. They are included as a reference to that limitless source of inspiration—nature.

All of the photographs are by Thomas Liden. Having studied pottery himself, he is sensitive to its qualities, and I feel that he has succeeded in making pictures of clarity and distinction.

I am indebted to Ed Germain for many helpful suggestions.

This book would have been a much lesser thing without the collaboration of my wife Lillyan. We worked together closely on the text and the illustrations, and she contributed many valuable insights which led to additions and clarifications.

Daniel Rhodes
Davenport, California

1 FORM

THE SHAPE AND STRUCTURE

Pottery forms, as they developed in the past and as they are still to a large extent today, seem quiet, restrained, centered, inward. They have a generalized as well as a particular character. The form of pots has sometimes been subservient or submissive to decoration and color, at least in those eras which followed the invention of glazes. While pottery has shared many values with sculpture, it is not sculpture, having as it does a functional dimension and projecting an image which is only subliminally, if at all, concerned with the depiction or abstraction of other forms. The pot has tended to remain a pot, without pretensions to high art, significance outside itself, or overt symbolism. Because of its subtleties, pottery form may not reveal itself fully at first. It usually does not crash into one's consciousness like, say, an African mask or a cathedral gargoyle. But with acquaintance, perhaps with use, a pot can grow on one, and the curve of a bowl or the neck and lip of a pitcher may be felt to belong to that realm of right form, form which has been generated from genuine feeling as against sentiment or programmed aesthetic. The pot may have an ineffable presence, a mysterious quality that makes it energized and reactive with its surroundings. Certainly not all pots have this. But enough do to demonstrate the power and the reality of simple clay forms.

THE SUBSTANCE

Clay is an extremely paradoxical material. During its plastic phase it is soft, slippery, impressionable, wet, easily worked or coaxed into almost any shape. Dry, it becomes chalklike, with a rather dead and lifeless quality and extreme fragility. After the first light fire, the clay becomes bone-like; absorbent but tough, with a return of a certain earthiness reminiscent of soft rock. Then, after the intense maturing fire, the clay is transformed into a rock-like substance, hard, brittle, dense, colored by the heat and flame, vulcanized as it were, and if in the form of a bowl, having a clear bell-like ring

1

when struck, quite an extraordinary property when one considers the original state of the plastic clay.

At no point in the mining, processing, mixing, and preparation of clay could it be said to have any distinct form of its own. It is either lumps, dust, watery slip, slurry, plastic mass, dried mass, or fired mass. Whatever form it assumes results from an outside force of some sort. Most materials from which things are made have some inherent form. Wood comes as trees or boards. Cloth is first fiber, then thread or yarn, then woven structure. Even metals came originally from nuggets or nodules which were beaten into shape or cast. Most materials resist change and have to be sawed, chiseled, hammered, beaten, or forced into the desired shapes. But clay is supine and nonresistant—it is moved by the gentlest squeeze or flattened by the merest pressure of the palm. It gives. Although it may become like stone when fired, in its original state it is the antithesis of stone. The form of pottery, then, is in no way given in the material. The soft plastic clay gives no hint of jars, cups, or pitchers.

Animal architecture predates man in its use of clay, notably in the nests of the mud wasp and of certain birds. In some unknown way, the birds and insects made the same discovery that men later made; that clay can be shaped to almost any desired form. The form, however, comes from the head. A canoe is a log which has been hollowed out, clothing is animal skin molded to human form, clubs are the broken off limbs of trees, a bow is a sapling blowing in the breeze, but a pot is a pristine form. Clay lay in the earth in a formless condition for millions of years before the wasp hit on the method of building nests with it and before man shaped it into a vessel.

Since forms in clay are conceived by man and there exists no prototype or direction in the material itself, they have always had a peculiarly intimate and human quality. The imagination and the touch of the hand are always felt. Each pottery form, created out of the soft and amorphous clay, is unique; it represents a fresh encounter between the potter and the clay.

The forms which pottery has assumed were evolved largely in response to demands of function. As we consider the various types such as bowls or pitchers, the shape will be analyzed in terms of these functional demands. Such an analysis may account for some of the broad features of the design, such as height in relation to width or size of the opening, but it cannot account for the more subtle qualities, those which grow out of the nuances. The method by which the piece was made is another factor in the form. Pieces made on the potter's wheel will have a different kind and quality of form than those which are built by coiling or modelling. The form thus grows out of process as well as in direct response to function.

2 WEDGING & KNEADING

PREPARATION

In pottery-making, the material must be prepared to a greater extent than in many other crafts, where the material may come by the yard or the board foot and needs only to be cut, carved, bent, or manipulated. Clay must not only be mixed together from various earthy ingredients which make up the body of it and be combined with water; it must also be tempered by the manipulative process of kneading or wedging. This tempering is necessary to bring about a true consistency within the material so that no part of the clay is stiffer or softer than any other part. It is also necessary in order to remove any air which exists within the clay mass, either as pockets of air or as frothy air within the grain of the clay. Also, in wedging, hard lumps or impurities (and sometimes, in the classroom, sponges, tools, or hairpins) may be discovered and removed. Wedging also brings about a mysterious springiness in the clay, perhaps associated with increased density.

VARIOUS METHODS

Most of the tempering can be done mechanically by the pug mill, which forces the clay through a nozzle and at the same time compacts it and removes the air. The pug mill is not a new device. Mule-driven mills were used in early American pottery shops. They were vertical drums with blades inside which revolved as the mule walked in a circle and forced the clay downward through an opening at the bottom. Pugged clay can be worked directly on the potter's wheel, but most potters prefer to wedge their clay by hand even if it has been first pugged and de-aired. Hand-wedging seems to give the clay an orientation and a life lacking in the mechanically prepared clay.

Clay to be wedged should be softer than needed for the processes of throwing, modeling, coil building, or slab building, because the wedging process removes moisture from the mass, stiffening it. This is especially true if the wedging is done on a plaster-surfaced table. Plaster, although widely used as a wedging surface, is not very satisfactory. It is usually either too dry or too wet, and small bits of plaster often come loose and get in the clay, causing firing flaws later in the finished piece.

The best surface for wedging is a low sturdy table with a top made of

3

two-by-eight soft wood planks. Wood has just the right absorbency to keep the clay from sticking to it. It dries quickly and is easy to clean. The table should be at the level of the knuckles of the hands when standing. If wood is found to retain too much moisture, and this could be the case if the wedging table is in constant use, the surface can be covered with a stretched piece of canvas.

A lump of clay about the size of a football is a convenient size for wedging. Very small pieces are hard to handle. Because of their weight, very large ones are too. But skill counts here more than brute strength. A scene in the famous film of the Sakuma pottery in Japan, taken before World War II when the village of Mashiko was truly a folk-pottery center, shows a slight girl dressed in a spotless kimono wedging a ball of clay which from appearance must have weighed at least forty pounds. She rolls the clay out into a long loaf, then upends it and repeats with another roll. Even for the skilled potter, wedging takes much energy, more than any other process in the craft. It is the start of action toward making pots, and it is in wedging that the potter senses his material, takes possession of it, and begins to develop rapport with it. Time at the wedging table can be a time for visualizing the finished work. Images and ideas arise from the cool moist clay on the palms and fingers. Wedged clay becomes personalized, and some potters avoid throwing balls of clay which have been wedged by someone else. Of course, in former times the apprentices did the wedging. An old ball of wedged clay seems to have lost something. Having been wrapped up and kept for a day or two, it will not have the same feel as a freshly wedged piece. Some kinetic potential seems to reside in the wedged ball of clay, more especially in one wedged by an accomplished potter. The shapes that the clay assumes during the wedging process also seem to presage the shapes of the pots; sloppy, ragged wedging often results in sloppy pots, and the firm, compact, simple shapes given to the clay during wedging by an expert seem to hold the promise of well-formed pots.

DIFFERENT TECHNIQUES

The actual techniques of wedging are simple enough. But, mysteriously, genuine ease and grace in the process seem to come slowly, often at about the same pace as the development of skill and art in wheel work, even though throwing is a much more complex thing to learn. The term wedging probably refers to the cutting and recombining of a loaf of clay, "wedging" the two halves together. The clay is formed into a neat shape by slamming it repeatedly on the table until it is shaped like a loaf of bread. Cutting is done on a stretched wire at the wedge table. The repeated cutting and recombining eliminates lumps and inconsistencies and eventually all air bubbles reach the surface and are eliminated. When the two halves are united, their

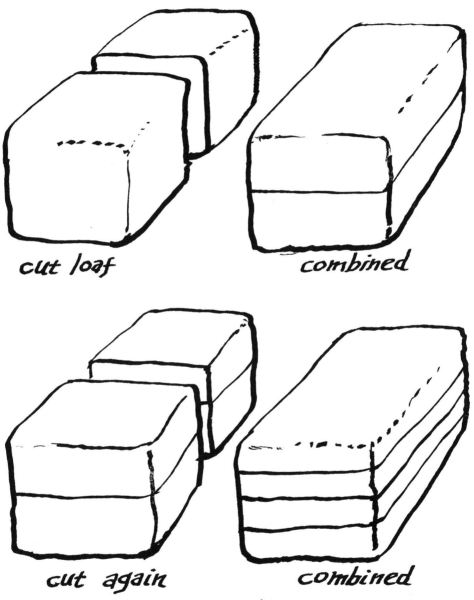

cut loaf   combined

cut again   combined

Fig. 1   Wedging.

surfaces must be quite smooth, otherwise air will be trapped between them (Figures 1 and 3).

For eliminating lumps, large grains, and frothy air the clay is sometimes pushed out onto the table with the heel of the hand, taking a little at a time from the lump and ending with a flattened form (Figure 4). Since this action leaves the clay in a spread-out irregular shape it must be followed by other kinds of wedging to bring about compaction.

Wire-cutting and wedging are usually followed by kneading or spiral wedging. In kneading, the clay is again formed into a loaf, which is then manipulated by the hands and especially the heels of the hands to make it roll onto itself in a form like a jelly roll. This rolling action produces what potters call the "ram's head," a name suggested by the appearance in the clay of what seems to be an animal face with horns (Figure 2). Sometimes, if the kneading is done in the right spirit, the face assumes a broad smile. The kneaded roll tends to get longer and longer, and at a certain point it is upended and the process repeated. Care must be taken not to trap air. This method of kneading does not involve picking the clay up off the table, and therefore requires relatively little effort.

Spiral wedging is a very efficient method, but it is difficult to master. The ball of clay is squeezed with the heel of one hand, then given a light turn and squeezed again (Figure 5). Either the right hand or the left hand may be used to exert the pressure. The clay is forced by the squeezing and the turning into a spiral pattern. As the clay is pressed out against the surface of the table, air pockets are eliminated. Spiral wedging is thought by some to orient the clay particles into circular patterns about a central point and thus to prepare the clay for the action of wheel throwing. Since the clay remains on the table, large pieces of clay can be conveniently handled by spiral wedging. Some potters prefer to wedge very large lumps on the floor. Spiral wedging is continuous and rhythmical, and it results in beautifully conditioned clay.

The form produced by spiral wedging is very flowing and energetic, a perfect record of the action (Figure 6). The method is called "chrysanthemum wedging" (*kiku-moni*) by Japanese potters, but to me the form suggests a sea shell more than it does a flower. The forms achieved in wedging are of course lost as the clay progresses toward its final shape, but one can think of these early wedged shapes as the metamorphic beginnings of pots. The wedged shapes, elemental as they are, presage the pot-to-be, and it augers well if they are compact and energized.

Fig. 2 Opposite top. *The "ram's head," formed by kneading the clay into a roll. Sometimes, when manipulated this way, the clay breaks into a smile.*
Fig. 3 Bottom. *Cut and recombined loaf of clay. The response of the clay to cutting and to the pressure of being slammed together indicates its readiness to be shaped.*

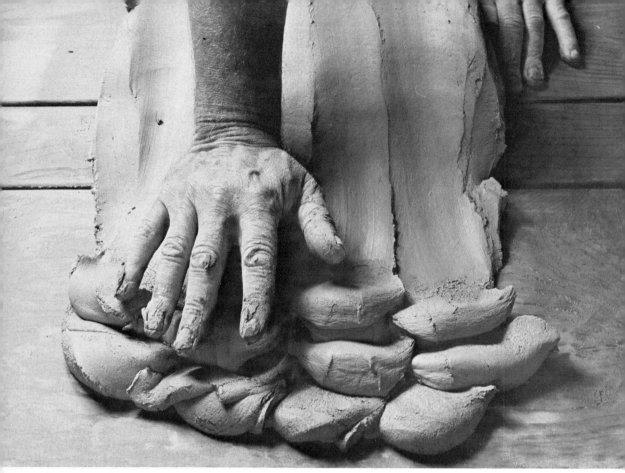

Fig. 4 Spreading the clay. This compacts the clay, squeezes out the air, and reveals lumps or foreign material.

Fig. 5 Opposite top. Spiral wedging. The left hand and arm are doing most of the work. The right hand turns the clay slightly between each squeeze.

Fig. 6 Bottom. Spiral-wedged clay. This method results in a form which perfectly reflects the rhythmic action of the arms and hands. The clay, traveling in a circular path, is de-aired and homogenized.

In Asia, wedging was sometimes done by treading on the clay with the foot. This process can still be observed in India at nonmechanized brick factories. The clay is pushed from one mass to another in stages, the effect being similar to the method shown in Figure 4. Since the weight of the entire body is above the foot, much force can be exerted.

How long to wedge? Too little wedging may result in failure at the wheel because of air pockets or lumps. On the other hand, prolonged wedging beyond a certain point is a waste of energy. The rule is long enough and then a little bit more.

Well-wedged clay acquires a feeling of density as the frothy texture caused by air is crushed out of it. It seems to respond to pressure and signals when it is ready to be shaped.

The wedged loaf of clay is cut into lumps of appropriate size for the pieces to be made. Some potters prefer to wedge each lump a bit more, giving it a compaction around its own center.

8

3 CENTERING

The wedged ball of clay is placed or thrown on the wheel head and patted down until its adhesion to the head is secure. Placing the ball initially as near to center as possible will be helpful to the beginner. The wheel head, if it is made of metal or wood should be clear of water or slip. If the head is plaster, it should be slightly damp, but not soaking wet. By patting the clay rhythmically with both hands as it slowly revolves, the clay can be brought toward center before the actual throwing begins (Figure 7). This patting of the clay to regularize its form and bring it to approximate center is especially useful for large pieces of clay.

The actual centering process begins with the wheel running fast and the ball of clay and the hands well lubricated with water. The spinning ball is grasped between the hands and pressure is applied from both sides (Figure 8). The hands and arms are steadied against the knees or against the pan of the wheel. As the clay revolves, its eccentricities meet with the relatively immobile surfaces of the palms and fingers, and with each revolution a smoothing and compression inward occurs. Some time is required for centering, some number of revolutions, no matter how expert the hands. Gradually the clay comes onto center.

A steady poised concentration is necessary. It is also necessary to exert sufficient force to overcome the irregularities of the clay. Often the main action of centering is done by one hand, usually the left, which pushes firmly against the spinning ball. The right hand may serve more as a guide. Centering can be done with one hand if the ball of clay is not too large, and to do this is a useful exercise in developing skill.

The key to rapid and accurate centering is to change the shape of the clay mass actively, as it revolves. As the spinning clay is forced to adapt to a new shape, it can no longer retain its original irregularity. If the clay is squeezed between the two palms and all the fingers it will grow upwards into a cone shape. Then, if pushed down from above by the palm of the right hand with the left hand serving as a guide at the sides, it will again assume its original shape, roughly a hemisphere. This process can be repeated several times;

each time will bring the clay nearer to perfect center. The clay can be raised to quite a narrow cone, and at this point, if the axis of the cone is made to lean or to bend slightly, the centering effect will be more pronounced (Figure 9). This is rather surprising; the clay form, spinning on its axis, is bent over a bit, but when the axis is allowed to become straight again the centering will be more perfect. When the clay is in the form of a relatively narrow cone, the tendency of the mass to take on a spiral orientation is more pronounced than if the clay is centered largely in the hemispheric state. This is said to facilitate hollowing and shaping. In the hemisphere stage, the clay should not be pushed down into too flat a form because of the difficulty of then raising it again without developing a hollow or dent in the top. The upper surface of the clay ball should always be rounded upwards. The clay should not splay out against the wheel head but should meet the head at approximately right angles. Otherwise it is difficult to coax the clay up again into a compact hemisphere.

The bald facts about centering are easily stated; throw a lump of clay down on the wheel, revolve it, squeezing between the wet hands until it is spinning smoothly under the palms. However, it does take much practice to master the operation. Difficulty comes not only from a lack of skill but from the condition of the clay. It must be well wedged, free from lumps or air pockets, and of the right consistency. Beginners should work with relatively soft clay, perhaps even with clay which is too soft to make a finished pot. Soft clay gives easily under the pressure of the hands and fingers, and thus gives the student a feel of what is needed to make the clay move. Insufficient speed or lack of lubrication, lack of decisive grip, unsteadiness of the hands or arms, nervous and erratic movement of the hands, and a lack of a sense of when the clay has actually reached center—all of these can lead to difficulty.

In centering, the hands and arms are held relatively motionless. Of course action is there, but it is in the form of quiet, steady, directed force, rather than in movement. The sensation is one of squeeze or grip on something which resists yet yields, pressure must be exerted to the point where the yielding begins but from there on much less force is needed. It is a matter of firm guidance. The potter learns to guide and to coax his clay. He is always alert through the sensations in his hands to what is happening to it. Vision has little or nothing to do with centering. It is a feeling. In mastering centering, the potter learns a basic attitude which is necessary in every phase of his craft. It is that one must respond to, respect, and learn to live with the nature of the clay. Nervous or quick movements must give way to a slower, steadier use of the hands and arms. The ends of the fingers and the palms must become sensitized and able to pick up the sometimes almost imperceptible signals from the clay. Pressure must be applied steadily and with finely gauged increments of either increase or decrease.

Pottery Form

As with many skills, once centering has been learned one wonders how it could have been at first so difficult. In the beginning the clay seems to resist centering and its eccentricities are devilishly persistent. Later, when things are going better, one senses that the clay is moving almost by itself toward center and only needs a gentle directing. One must collaborate with it; the clay must not be opposed with too much force. The action is one of

Fig. 7   Slapping the clay on center. This preliminary centering is helpful, especially for large lumps of clay.

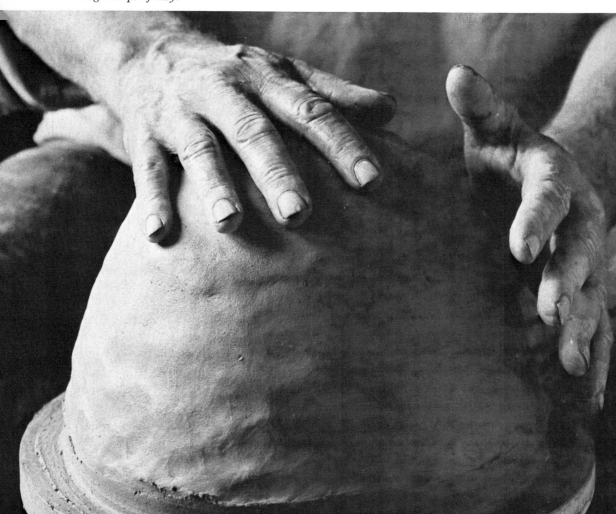

concentration inward. The gestures of the body, the arms, and the hands are all directed toward the quiet and the stillness of the axis. This axis in the clay can actually be felt as a sensation if the end of the thumb is placed on its North pole.

In centering, the clay moves from the formless to the formed. Symmetry, order, and the potential for growth suddenly appear.

Fig. 8 Centering. The clay is formed into an almost perfect hemisphere.
Fig. 9 Overleaf. Centering. Forcing the clay up into a cone and then lowering it again into a hemisphere helps to bring it onto perfect center.

4 HOLLOWING OUT

The ball of clay spinning on the wheel on perfect center is a creation of the potter and is under his control. It is not a pot. It retains its solidity, its density, its earthy globular form. With hollowing, the clay begins to evolve into the world of enclosed space.

Once centering is mastered, hollowing out the form will come rather easily. The speed of the wheel is reduced somewhat. The finger or thumb is placed at the exact top of the hemisphere and a depression is started by a slight pressure, rather shallow at first and kept filled with water for lubrication. The fingers probe downward, following the axis, which is consumed by the developing hollow. The hollow at first takes the form more of a conical depression than a drilled hole. The clay seems to part rather easily at its true center, and if skillfully done, hollowing will not much disturb the centered symmetry of the mass.

As the probing fingers press downward toward the surface of the wheel head, a resistance is felt; what will be the bottom of the pot is being approached. From this developing resistance the potter gauges the thickness of the clay above the wheel head and makes his decision as to how thick the

Fig. 10   Development of the cylinder.

15

Fig. 11   Hollowing. When the clay is hollowed and spread, it assumes a doughnut-like form.

bottom should be. Then, with a spreading motion, the bottom of the interior is widened (Figure 11). The ball of clay suddenly becomes a vessel; thick, embryonic, unformed, but still a hollowed-out thing with the interior catching darkness. With the hollowing out of the ball, the potential of the clay is felt. It begins to respond more readily to gentle pressures and to move outward or inward as the hands urge.

Certain features of the hollowed-out ball portend a well-made pot. The sides are straight, or tending inward somewhat. The upper edge is sturdy, thick, and doughnut-like. The form meets the wheel head at a right angle, and all of the clay is available to be lifted up into the pot, rather than tending to spread out over the wheel head. The interior of the form is a simple cylinder with the bottom of the pot-to-be already established as to thickness and breadth. Even in the embryonic stage of a hollowed-out ball, the eventual form may be sensed; plate-like forms will already demand that the hollowed form be broad, while tall or narrow forms must be preceded by a preliminary doughnut which is narrow and tending strictly inward toward center.

16

Fig. 12   The start of a cylinder. A thickened upper edge is maintained and a slight inward direction. The sponge is used on the outside.

If the hollowing results in the clay becoming somewhat off center, the clay is first pressed inward, then outward, then slightly upward. These little changes are carried out with the whole of the hands, feeling for response and control. As in centering, taking the clay through subtle changes in form brings it back to center. The two hands play equal and similar roles; they press from without, probe for center, mold and shape.

5 THE CYLINDER

The hollowed-out ball must now be raised and made to grow into a pot. This seeming miracle is accomplished by the simple action of squeezing the wall of the spinning form between the fingers of the two hands, forcing the clay to move upwards. (Figure 10 shows the shapes the clay will take.) The left hand now moves to the interior while the right hand presses from the outside. Pressure is applied at the very bottom. On smaller pieces, the fingertips alone are used. On larger pieces, the knuckle of the forefinger may be used on the outside to give a broader area of pressure. Or the wet sponge may be used. The beginner, however, should practice without the sponge until he gets the feel of throwing and knows the kind and degree of pressure required. The question of how hard to press, and how fast to move up the cylinder can only be answered by experience, by getting a feel of the yielding clay and its movement upwards. Each pull must start at the bottom and continue to the top. There the fingers gather over the rim and caress the clay into a smooth running and slightly thickened lip (Figure 12). Too rapid an ascent will create a spiral screw in the cylinder, causing trouble in the next pull, while too slow a trip up the wall will get nowhere and the clay will become soggy from excessive wetting. Wetting must be carefully done before each pull. A squeezed sponge can dribble just enough water on the rim to spread over both the inside and the outside surfaces but not puddle excessively in the bottom or on the wheel head.

Each pull is a separate operation. Between pulls, water is applied and the wheel kicked to regain speed. The speed used in cylinder-making is very much slower than for centering and as the walls of the piece are thinned and the form is extended, the speed can be diminished. The acceleration or deceleration of the wheel, wetting, pulling up, and rim control will vary with the size and nature of the pot. A small bowl or cylinder may require only one or two pulls, while a large or complex piece will need many. Vision has little to do with the process. What counts is the feel of the turning clay and its subtle changes as felt through the fingers. One is really throwing when the clay is felt to grow in the hands and the cylinder is rising almost by itself.

A light tender touch on the clay and a feeling of response: this feedback tells us what is happening in the pot. The cylinder cannot be commanded or forced into existence: rather it grows in gentle collaboration between hands and clay. Each cylinder will rise to a point beyond which no further pull will cause it to rise higher. It seems to know when to stop growing.

The principal difficulty of cylinder-making, or in the making of any form on the wheel for that matter, is the tendency of the clay not to rise and to remain in the lower section. This produces the thick lower wall which is the mark of the amateur's pot. Long practice is required to overcome this. The lower part of the pot must be given special attention, and pressure applied until the clay is felt to move and there is response between the left and right hands.

Another difficulty is the tendency of the cylinder to spread outward into a bowl-like form. In experienced hands, the clay is prevented from doing this by a dominance of the outside hand, pushing in just enough to keep control and to counter the strong centrifugal force of the wheel. It is best if the cylinder is at first slightly tapered in toward the top. But if a splaying out or widening does occur, it can be corrected by gently collaring in the clay with the fingers held at widely separated points, constricting and narrowing the circumference until verticality is restored (Figure 13).

The well-made cylinder will have near straight sides, tapering in slightly toward the top. Its bottom inside will be flat, with no excess clay in the corner where the side meets the bottom. The wall will be of almost uniform thickness, having no more than a slight thickening toward the lower part of the form. The lip will be smooth, true, and thickened into a slight bead for reinforcement. From such a cylinder, an infinite number of shapes can develop. It is the ancestor form for wheel-made pots.

The freshly thrown pot is so wet, soft, and easily distorted that the thought of picking it up seems incongruous. Like picking up a baby, it must be done right; what looks so weak and fragile proves to be tougher than one would think.

First the pot must be cut loose from the wheel head. A wire made of two or three twisted strands is held tautly against the surface of the head of the slowly turning wheel. Before cutting, excess water must be sponged off the head, for if water runs in under the pot with the cut, it may prevent easy release. Then the wire is drawn under the pot, care being taken not to allow slack in the wire. Looking down inside the pot the ripple of the wire passing across the bottom can be seen, a sign that the bottom is not too thick. Different sizes and shapes require different approaches to lifting. Small pieces can be picked up by grasping them with the fingers at the bottom. Larger forms are grasped between the palms of the hands, spreading the contact as far as possible. The soft pot is carefully set down on the waiting ware board. Some distortion is inevitable, but even if the form becomes crooked as it is set

Fig. 13 Opposite top. *Collaring-in. The fingers and the thumbs press gently at four equidistant points, narrowing the cylinder.*
Fig. 14 Opposite bottom. *Swelling out the form. The form is expanded by pressure from the fingers of the hand inside. The right hand guides and controls the swelling.*
Fig. 15 *Making a narrow-necked form. This inward movement must be done slowly and gently, otherwise wrinkles and unevenness will develop.*

down, it tends to go back to its original symmetry as it dries. After an hour or so, the shape can be adjusted or corrected by slightly squeezing or tapping the pot.

Lifting a pot from the wheel will give an indication of the thrower's skill. If the pot is too soft to pick up, it means that too much water has been used, or that the piece has been on the wheel too long and been overworked.

The whorl on the bottom of a pot caused by the wire cutting through the slowly revolving clay is a beautiful detail which grows directly out of process. The pattern of lines tells of the revolving motion of the wheel, and also of the slowing and the termination of that motion. The bottom whorl can be seen on Minoan pots dating back to at least 1500 B.C.

The pot as it is lifted off the wheel may be completely finished and require no further trimming or shaping. This should be the goal of wheel practice; to acquire the ability to throw pieces which are immediately brought to final shape, are relatively stiff and tough enough to handle, and which have no excess clay in the lower walls or the bottom.

6 FORM CHARACTERISTICS OF WHEEL-MADE POTTERY

What has been said so far about throwing is in a way an attempt to describe the indescribable. Any description of throwing misses the point, which is the actual feel of the clay as it evolves into a pot. The foregoing is intended more as a record of my own subjective feelings about throwing than as a detailed instruction. I realize that there is little I can say about the actual touch on the clay, which is of course the heart of the process.

Most fabricating techniques involve taking some material and adding a bit of it at a time until the form appears. Building a boat, weaving cloth, or stringing beads. Or, fabrication may be accomplished by taking away, as in carving wood or stone. Casting of metals or plastic involves making a negative which is actually a completed version of the form before the final material is dealt with. Forging, hammering, or spinning metals is closer to wheel throwing, but these are slow processes and the hand is used to power and to guide tools rather than directly.

The potter at the wheel manipulates the material as a whole and transforms the lump of clay into a pot. The pot under his hand grows in an organic fashion, starting out as a primal, thick cylinder and flowering out from that to its final form. The process does not involve either addition or subtraction of material.

Other processes of shaping clay, such as coil building and modeling, are additive. The exception is the direct modeling of an object or a vessel from one lump of clay, which does have much in common with throwing.

Throwing, then, is a rather unique process. Not only is the material managed directly in the hands and guided from the formless to the formed, but this process is fast and uninterrupted. No prior visualization or design of the form is necessary. The action and the form it creates are as one. Thought need not intervene between the action of the fingers, the hands, the eyes, and the realization of the form. I do not mean to imply that throwing is an automatic or thoughtless process—thought may enter in the conceptualization of the form and later in its evaluation. But it is true that throwing, perhaps more than any other craft, is a direct, immediate expression. The form is generated, not designed. Design means "to mark out." But pots

22

are not marked out beforehand—they grow on the wheel in response to movement, action, pressures, feelings. Small wonder that throwing on the wheel exerts a fascination and attraction which goes beyond the mere desire to make pots. It is one of those rare areas of activity where intent and deed are as one.

Pots are quickly made on the wheel. This can result in rather sketchy, spontaneous forms. A certain informality and perhaps surprise can be there. No two pieces will ever be exactly alike, although of course production shops in times past have approached the uniformity of mass production. Since no great amount of time need be invested in any one pot, and since the material need only be wedged up again to be reused, each piece can be treated rather casually. It is no great loss if the pot collapses—if it does not please, away with it. Throwing pots can be just an exercise in forming, a trying out of one's particular powers to shape, and need not result in any finished work at all. Throwing, at least as the pot nears completion, is an encounter with very soft clay, softer than the clay used for modeling, coiling, or slabs. Thrown clay is therefore more responsive to the nuances of touch than clay worked in any other way.

The wheel-made pot will be more or less symmetrical. If the clay departs too much from the symmetrical, it cannot really be further manipulated on the wheel. Thus all thrown pots are in one family of form—the circle—and the variations come from variations in profile only. (Here I am excluding those distortions which may be given to pots after they leave the wheel, which are discussed in section 22, Altering and Combining Thrown Forms.) This narrowing of the possibility of variation in form may be felt as a severe limitation if one takes a sculptural approach to working clay. To make only forms which are symmetrical about a central axis may seem a giving up of many tempting possibilities. But viewed positively, the restrictions on form conferred by the wheel may furnish a framework, a defined area in which forms can generate in a certain way without diffusion into a world of unlimited possibilities. Our urges to *form,* to shape a material (or a space) are normally the outgrowth of specific conditions such as material, time, place, functional purpose, prior models, and, of course, the quality of imagination brought to the task. To face a polymorphous material like clay and to move it without the limitation of any concept is perhaps impossible. What I mean is that we are always working within real limitations, and that using the wheel to shape clay is just one form of limitation. Accepting the limitation is not necessarily a loss. It is just moving within a somewhat defined area, accepting a ground on which to work. Looked at in this way, all sculptural shaping of materials involves a "giving up." One form, or one approach to form, as exemplified in a shaped object, precludes all others.

The thrown pot, although it is essentially symmetrical about an axis, may show departures from this axis in the form of crookedness, waywardness of form, eccentricity. But these irregularities tend to be aberrations, and their presence may even reinforce the sense of symmetry. A crookedness which is a departure from symmetry is different from growths of form in an object which is essentially asymmetrical.

Symmetry in pottery produces an even and circular upper edge that tends to establish a certain calm resolution to the form. As they are made, thrown pots develop from a lump of clay on a flat base. The clay moves upward. The mass of material must be moved from below up into the walls of the pot. This feeling of a flat platform as the basis of the form frequently persists in the finished pot. Trimming or adding feet may give the piece a lift, but the throwing process itself tends to produce stable, rooted forms.

Thrown pottery has a surface texture which results from the process. It is not something added on. Unless taken off by trimming or scraping or by the use of ribs, there will be throwing marks both inside and outside. These marks—by their prominence, scale, and rhythm—record the action of the hands and tell of the pressures and gestures which produced the form.

7 CYLINDRICAL FORMS

In this and later sections I will be discussing basic pottery forms. These are actually rather few in number; but they have been extraordinarily durable through the centuries and have been produced by many cultures. One can generalize about these forms only up to a point; and it must be kept in mind that the actuality of the art of pottery rests on unique, individual pots, not on classes or species of forms. Nevertheless, a consideration of those few types of forms which have become common, and around which variations cluster, may be helpful in understanding pottery form in its fundamentals.

As they are produced on the wheel, almost all thrown pots develop from a cylinder. The cylinder thus is a kind of embryo form which grows into various final shapes. But the cylinder also has a life of its own. From the study of cylinders, one can discover some important things about the form of pottery. One realizes that subtle variations in form often make a great deal of difference in the final result. If a thrown cylinder were perfectly straight-sided, it would have no more interest as a form than a section of cut-off pipe. But the potter soon learns that clay, in whatever process it is worked, resists the straight line or the flat plane, and even if one succeeded in making a perfect cylinder, it would likely change during drying and firing so that its sides would have some undulation, perhaps very subtle but nevertheless enough to remove it from the category of mechanically shaped objects. As this variation from the exactly geometric occurs, and as it is encouraged both consciously and subconsciously by the potter, the cylinder is moved into another realm, a shaped form, a form with movement and rhythm.

The cylinder which tends inward at the top, which becomes in effect a truncated cone, tightens the hold on the space inside. Liquids contained inside will be less likely to splash and vision to the inside is reduced, even if only slightly, giving a deeper mystery to the interior. The feeling of such a shape tends toward tightness, constriction, and tidiness of form.

The cylinder tending outward has the reverse emphasis. Its interior is more accessible and visible. It is receptive to content and more willingly gives up content. The glaze or surface of the inside gains more exposure and becomes more important. The form moves not only upwards but slightly outward, like a growing plant.

The barrel-shaped cylinder has the beginnings of rotundity, no matter how slight the outward curve. The interior space has taken on a more active,

palpable quality. It is taut at the top and at the bottom but swelling and relaxed through the middle. Its top rim is a repeat, or memory of the bottom circumference. In making the barrel shape, the potter is conscious of the dominance of the left inside hand as the form develops through the middle, and then of the constricting influence of the right hand at the top.

The cylinder with a slightly concave wall seems to be reaching upwards, stretching. Its interior space is dominated by the wall, structurally strong and pressing inward. The concave wall seems to support decoration well, as exemplified by Persian and Hispano-Mooresque drug jars. These essentially cylindrical pieces with slightly concave sides were perhaps made that way to facilitate picking up and handling.

The character of the simple cylinder, then, depends on the subtle emphasis of the form either inward or outward to form a taper, a swelling out, or a constriction. This play between inner and outer forces is enacted by the two hands. The left hand is in charge of the inside. It expresses and defines the pot's space. The right hand, pressing from the outside, controls, directs, and defines the pot's form. The exact shape is not conferred by the left hand. It pushes outward in a rather generalized gesture, and it remains for the outside hand to furnish the focus, the proportion, the "drawing" of the form. These two forces at work in the birth of a pot, inside-outside, left-right, space-contour, swelling-constriction are the "Yin and Yang" of the wheel. The inside force, is, of course the Yin, the earth force (*chi*) the generative principle, the feminine polarity. The outside is Yang, the active, masculine principle.

Vitality in pottery form seems to arise out of the simultaneous interaction and the collaboration of these forces. Their union results in the form in which right and left, inside and outside are polarities rather than separate entities, intrinsically related as the two ends of a stick are to the whole stick (Figures 16 through 20).

Fig. 16 Opposite. *Cylindrical form. The tool marks and indentations give a sense of both the motion of the wheel and the action of the hand.*

Fig. 17 Overleaf, left to right. *Cylindrical form. The rather formal shape is relieved and complemented by the tool marks and the indentation.*

Fig. 18 *Cylindrical form. A rather soft form with a collar, given indentations with a wooden rib. Although essentially cylindrical, the profile below the collar makes a slow S curve. The bottom was rounded by rolling on the table.*

Fig. 19 *Cylindrical form. This piece was thrown very quickly, with no attempt made to "clean it up." The prominent throwing marks result from a vigorous last pull which shaped as well as raised the pot. A dent remains from lifting the piece off the wheel.*

Fig. 20 *Cylindrical form. A rapidly thrown, untrimmed piece with a simple drum shape. The indented lines in the clay on the outside and the lip overhanging the interior move it somewhat away from a simple geometric form.*

8 TOOLS FOR THROWING

The hands are the real tools of the craft, and little else besides the wheel is required for throwing. The simplicity of the process in terms of tools contrasts to its unusually rich and complex involvement with coordination, sensory perception, gut feeling, and intellect. Except for the wheel, all of the required tools are simple, readily available, or easily made (Figures 21 and 22).

HISTORY OF THE POTTER'S WHEEL

The potter's wheel itself could be the subject of a book. It is one of the oldest mechanical devices, going back to at least 2000 B.C. It undoubtedly developed from a revolving platform of some sort used to facilitate hand building or coil building. But it is actually a big step from the turntable or modeling stand to the potter's wheel. The process of throwing, involving as it does the shaping of a pot from one lump of clay, is fundamentally different from hand building by additions of clay, and to be effective, the wheel must have considerable momentum to counter the friction of the hands on the clay, and must run true at speeds up to 120 RPM. It is my guess that throwing was an invention, rather than a slow development or refinement of earlier hand-building techniques. The invention of throwing speeded up the production of pottery and made possible light, highly symmetrical pieces and near perfect duplicates. The potter's wheel apparently was first used in Egypt. Egyptian wall pictures tell of its existence but they are not explicit as to design or operation and in fact may actually represent something more akin to modeling stands. Ancient Egyptian pots indicate that rapidly turning, well-centered wheels existed and that the techniques of throwing were more or less identical to those in use today. Minoan pots at least as old as 1500 B.C. demonstrate that just about every wheel technique was then in use. There are rims, lids, handles, trimming, sectional pieces, added feet, deliberate distortions to the thrown shape, and wheel-made sculpture. Large storage jars were made by first throwing the lower section of a jar, then adding large coils of clay, each coil being thrown in turn to add to the form. In 1966 I saw potters

29

Pottery Form

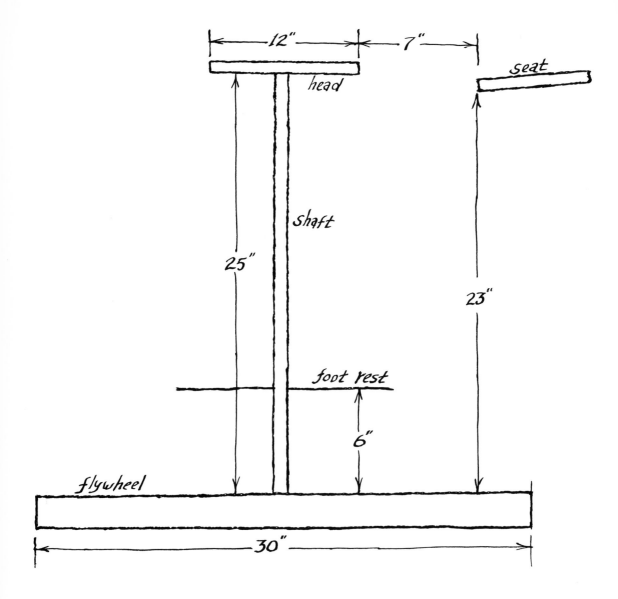

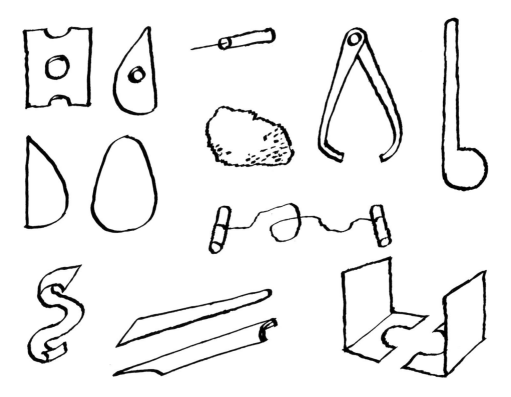

Fig. 21   Opposite. *Approximate dimensions of the wheel.*
Fig. 22   *Throwing tools.*

in Crete using this same technique for olive curing jars. The potter worked outdoors on five primitive wheels. On each wheel was a jar in process, and he added a large coil to each pot in turn. When the last coil had been thrown, the first pot was dry enough to receive another coil. In form, the jars were almost identical to those which may be seen in the grain storage area at the ancient Palace of Knossos.

Knowledge of the potter's wheel spread from Egypt and Crete to Greece. The Myceneans, precursors of the Greeks, were master potters. Their swelling, beautifully proportioned jars are an evidence of great virtuosity on the wheel. For the Greeks, pottery-making became a large scale industry and perhaps for this reason the forms of Greek pottery eventually became mechanical and repetitious. Greek pots were usually trimmed overall to establish the final form, and there is little feeling in them of throwing as a process. Profile seems to dominate over volume, and the pot became more a prop for decoration than a form which had any life of its own.

The Romans developed the press-mold as a major method of pottery-making but continued to use the wheel also. They established potteries throughout their colonies in France, Britain, Germany, and Spain and archeological remains indicate large scale production. Knowledge of the wheel thus spread throughout Europe.

The wheel itself was never discovered in America. Lacking this primary device, the potter's wheel could hardly have been conceived of. But in spite of the fact that none of the pottery of the various pre-Columbian cultures was wheel-made, there is a remarkable similarity in ceramic technique between these pots and the early pots of Europe, Africa, and Asia. The art of pottery—including shaping, tempering clay, decorating in colored slips, polishing, making handles, feet, knobs, and so forth, as well as sculpturing of effigy jars, and the like—was somehow invented independently in the Americas.

Wheel-made pots were produced in China at least as early as 1500 B.C., perhaps much earlier. Whether the knowledge of throwing came from the Mediterranean area to China, or whether the potter's wheel was invented separately cannot be known. Probably, it was imported. We know nothing of the design of early Chinese pottery wheels but, judging from the pots, it must have been essentially like those of the West. Expertly thrown Chinese pots in some cases imitated bronze forms and in other cases seem to have been the inspiration for bronzes. During over three thousand years of development, almost every imaginable variation on wheel technique was practiced by the Chinese.

Korean and Japanese throwing developed much later than the art in China and derives from it. The Koreans used a very light kick wheel with little momentum, and this may account for the irregularity of many Korean pots. The Japanese, preferring to work sitting down in a cross-legged position, developed a wheel which combines the flywheel and the head in a large rather heavy disk mounted on a bearing. This is activated by a stick which is placed in a notch in the wheel head and twirled by a motion of the wrist. Since it is more convenient to twirl in a clockwise, rather than counterclockwise direction, Japanese wheels came to run in the opposite direction to those used elsewhere. When the wheel is running clockwise, the right hand is used inside the pot and the left hand on the outside, the reverse of our practice. The fact that the Japanese could make pots this way seems to support the idea that the two hands play an equal part in throwing. Left-handed throwers ordinarily do not reverse the role of the hands, but throw in the same manner as the right handed.

In India, the wheel is constructed like a top. It has a wide, heavy head and a short shaft with a single bearing below. Only when spinning does it stand with the turning wheel horizontal to the ground. The Indian wheel seems an awkward device since the potter must lean in over the wide wheel to reach the spinning clay and there is no support for wrists or arms. But pots are produced on these wheels with seeming ease and certainly with speed. The design of the Indian wheel is perhaps attributable to the need of itinerate potters to have a wheel which is easy to move from place to place—it has no frame.

THE WHEEL TODAY

Perhaps the best type of wheel is the kick wheel with a heavy circular flywheel. This wheel has many advantages. The effort required for kicking can be concentrated between periods of working on the pot, all throwing being done during the momentum phase when the foot is at rest. The slowing down of the wheel corresponds to the natural need to slow down in the manipulation of the clay. Therefore, the action of the wheel and what is happening to the pot on the wheel are in phase in a natural way. On the other hand, the treadle wheel, requiring a busy and incessant motion of the bar, demands constant attention from the foot. Wheels powered mechanically have essentially no relationship between their mechanisms, the methods of controlling them, and what is actually happening in throwing.

The *kick wheel* is a simple device. A smooth head of metal or wood about 12 inches in diameter is mounted on a shaft with a collar bearing above and a thrust bearing below. The flywheel is usually about 30 inches in diameter and

Fig. 23   Overleaf left. *Vase. The chimney-like neck is an important element. The form, from bottom to top, is made up of swellings alternating with changes of direction.*
Fig. 24   Overleaf right. *Jar. The body of the jar is accented at the bottom by a sturdy foot and at the top by a neck and collar. The inward curving line at the collar serves to complement the swelling, positive form of the body, and a play is created between distension and constriction.*

Fig. 25 Below. Jar. Two very simple elements make up this pot; a swelling, almost globular, body and a cylindrical neck.

Fig. 26 Opposite top. Jar. This large piece was made with the Korean technique of adding wide ribbons of clay, throwing each in turn to complete the form. The joints are still somewhat evident.

Fig. 27 Opposite bottom. Vase. The form sweeps out drastically and returns to a small neck.

Fig. 28 Overleaf left. Vase. Very quickly thrown, this piece retains its rather heavy throwing marks and slightly crooked profile. The form is undulating rather than precise.

Fig. 29 Overleaf top right. Jar. Although basically a cylinder, the form has movement created by the constriction at the top, the throwing marks, the flattened area, and a sweeping groove made with a wooden tool.

Fig. 30 Overleaf bottom right. Jar. The mobile and rather tremulous form results from rapid throwing on a slow-turning wheel.

the same speed when the work actually demands either slowing down or speeding up. Perhaps the worst drawback of power wheels is the noise they make. They whine, groan, clank, or knock. The noise intrudes on what otherwise is a silent craft. Clay-working does have a quiet and contemplative quality about it; to preserve that from the intrusions of noisy machines is worth something.

Probably the best power wheel is the kick wheel which has a regular flywheel which can be either kicked or activated by a motor. This gives all of the advantages of the kick wheel plus the benefits of power. The motor is used when centering, and for the more delicate operations of shaping the wheel runs on momentum.

RIBS

Throwing can be done entirely with the hands, but various ribs are used to control, refine, or finish the surface. The ribs may be of two types: wooden and flexible metal. The wooden ribs are used on the outside of the pot; they are primarily useful to widen the area of contact with the wall of the pot and thus apply the pressure over a broader area than that furnished by the fingers or knuckles. The wet rib is held against the spinning clay and the inside fingers work against it. The rib will require less water for lubrication than the fingers. These wooden ribs are made in different shapes. The straightedged rib is used when the form is being directed toward a straight sided or cylindrical profile. Rounded ribs function more like the knuckle. The use of wooden ribs may introduce a somewhat mechanical quality into the form. The clay conforms to the surface of the rib rather than being guided by the finger. Furthermore, the rib eliminates throwing marks, leaving an essentially smooth surface. That is, in fact, one of the main purposes of the rib.

Ribs made of flexible steel have a different function. Held on the outside, the rib can be bent to conform somewhat to the bulge of a bowl or jar. Another metal rib can be held inside. The two metal ribs used this way are more for shaping than for thinning. They tend to scrape off the throwing marks and water from the sides of the pot; if the pot is finished with ribs, it may be stiffer and easier to pick up than a pot done with only fingers and sponge. Controlling the form of a piece between two ribs is a skill in itself, and one must learn how much pressure to apply. The use of metal ribs for shaping can result in very neat and precise work. But as in the case of wooden ribs, the result can be rather dead and mechanical. The profile curves possible with the bent metal rib on the outside are severely limited.

For most work, the best practice seems to be the use of the sponge on the outside and the fingers on the inside. Details—such as sharp corners, precisely defined beads at the lip, or circumference lines—can be added with the rib or modeling tool. Any technique which removes the intimate contact of hand to pot will tend to deaden the flow of energy and feeling into the clay.

A useful tool for making pieces with a swelling profile, especially narrow-necked pieces, is the inside wooden tool as shown in Figure 22. The curved head of the tool is held on the inside of the pot as a substitute for the hand and is used to exert outward pressure. With this tool, the pot can still be bellied out even if the opening is too small to admit the hand.

9 JARS & VASES

The term jar refers to a vessel which is used for storage and has a wide enough opening for easy access. A vase is not necessarily different in shape from a jar, but the word implies a more ornamental use, or use as a container for flowers. Vessels with quite narrow openings may be termed vases.

The jar is the elemental pottery form. With the birth of pottery as a craft, it was one of the first forms to emerge. It was made first by modeling or coiling, later on the potter's wheel. The form appears in all pottery-making cultures, and all other pottery forms could be considered derivations from it. To appreciate the importance of the pottery jar and its function, we must imagine the world as it was, without metals or plastic. The materials from which containers could be fashioned were limited: wood, stone, leather, fiber. Wood was hard to shape, apt to split, and until the development of cooperage was little used for vessels. (The large cooking tubs of wood made by the American Indians of the northwest coast are an exception. The tub was first filled with cold water. Then hot rocks were put in, bringing the water to a boil for cooking.) Stone was almost impossible to hollow out into a vessel and was heavy. Leather or skin, except bladders, was hard to make into a waterproof container and was subject to attack by rodents. Baskets too could be gnawed through and, unless woven with extremely fine and closely worked reed, were not waterproof. The pottery jar filled an urgent need. It was used for the storage of food, water, grain, and seed. It provided protection from moisture, insects, and rodents. It could be made with relative ease and, if broken, could be replaced.

According to Lewis Mumford, "the great fact about neolithic technics is that its main innovations were not in weapons and tools but in containers. Paleolithic tools and weapons were addressed to movements and muscular efforts . . . but in woman the soft internal organs are the center of her life; her arms and legs serve less significantly for movement than for holding and enclosing, whether it be a lover or a child; and it is in the orifices and sacs, in mouth, vulva, vagina, breast, womb, that her sexually individualized activities take place. Under woman's dominance, the neolithic period is pre-eminently

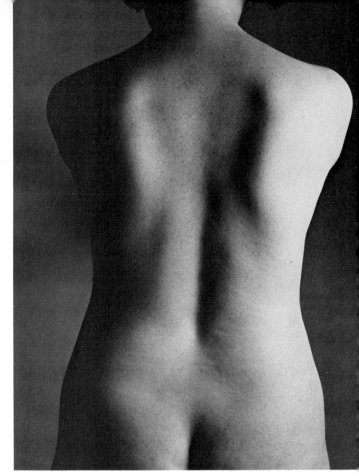

Fig. 31 Torso.

one of containers; it is an age of stone and pottery utensils, of vases, jars, vats, cisterns, bins, barns, granaries, houses. . . ." (From Lewis Mumford, *The City in History,* Harcourt, Brace & World, Inc., New York, 1961, p. 15–16.)

The basic elements of the jar, a sturdy base, a swelling midsection, and an open but somewhat constricted neck have been interpreted by potters in an infinite number of variations. The advent of throwing did not alter the essentials of the form.

On the wheel, the jar grows rather naturally and easily out of the cylinder. The cylinder can be thought of as a kind of blank from which the final form is made. The bottom of the cylinder is given the final thickness and diameter of the finished piece. The cylinder needs to be quite narrow, even if a widely swelling piece is projected, for only in the form of a cylinder can the clay be effectively thinned and raised. Once the jar is formed, its walls will slump if further thinning is attempted.

With the wheel turning slowly, the widening pulls are made. Starting from the bottom, the left hand pushes out gently, urging the clay into a wider shape as it comes up (Figure 14). The right hand guides, restrains, and measures the swelling but exerts little pressure or force. The dark hollow of the pot gains volume with each upward travel of the hands. The hands may travel

44

downward also, starting with the neck or collar and pushing outward to form the shoulder and belly. The opening is kept narrow, just wide enough to admit the hand. This process of widening and shaping does not raise the clay upwards or increase the height of the piece. In fact, the height will decrease as the girth grows. Stretching out the wall of the pot requires very little pressure compared to the action required to raise the cylinder.

When the desired width or profile of the shoulder and belly of the piece has been achieved, the upper part of the form is collared in and constricted to form the neck. The tips of the fingers grasp the slowly turning form and gently squeeze it at equally separated points. As the clay comes in, the shoulder is defined. At this point, if the opening has become too narrow for the hand, the wooden profile tool can be used on the inside to widen or correct the

Fig. 32 Jar. The style of potting is loose. It was made on a very slow-turning wheel, with no attempt made to true up the profile.

Fig. 33 Group of thrown pots. Pieces like these, having no extremes of form, are easily and quickly made. Only the bowl was trimmed.

shape further. After this closing in, the interior will not feel the touch of the hands again. (At some later time when the pot meets the eventual fate of all pots, to be broken, the inside surface might be seen again.)

Collaring in will thicken the clay and from this thickened wall at the top the neck and lip are formed.

The two basic maneuvers of throwing, swelling out the form, and narrowing and restraining it are at the heart of the potter's art. The music of the wheel sounds in this undulation inward and outward, swelling and contracting. The function and spirit of the pottery jar thus takes shape. Its mass, dark, voluminous, and generating, is formed by the hand feeling and urging outward from center. The upper neck and lip constrains the volume below, holds and protects its contents, moving with elasticity back toward the central axis.

From an ample and sturdy base the walls of the jar rise. The form immediately reaches outward, curving, responding to the pressure of the space within. We speak of curves and profile, but what is happening is *volume.* The story of a pot is more related to the blowing up of a balloon than it is to the drawing of a shape on paper. The pot stretches to include the hollow within. Its shape is felt as a confinement of this hollow. The lower part of the vessel may have an element of straightness or stiffness to support the form above, countering any tendency toward drooping or slumping. The form moves upward and outward. At some moment the widest circumference is reached and the dynamic of growth is slowed in a flattened or stabilizing zone. Then the inward constriction begins, defining the shoulder. At this point, structure, order, and strength may be felt. What had started out below as a gentle billowing out of the form changes at the shoulder to control, inwardness, and the termination of the jar at the neck and lip (Figure 25).

The belly of the pot is space, undifferentiated and ready to receive. Perhaps we identify it with our own interior, ready to take whatever we ingest. In empathy, the neck of the jar is the tube of our throat. One can feel what is going down it. Its inside surfaces may still be experienced to a degree with eye or fingers. The neck of the jar, perhaps almost cylindrical, represents the resolution of the form, the return to the static feeling also expressed by the base (Figures 24 and 25). The neck of the jar may be short, sturdy, and strong, or it may be longer and narrower (Figures 23 and 28). These different openings have a bearing on how we feel about the inside of the piece, whether it is remote or accessible.

The rim or lip is the final accent, and the thickening of the clay here is a kind of punctuation mark. The lip may turn outward or downward slightly or it may be just a thickening bead.

Whereas the jar was made with the two hands working together but separated, one inside and one outside, the lip is finished with all eight fingers meeting and caressing the clay into a smooth-running finished circle. The base, the outward curving belly, the shoulder, the neck, and lip are now inseparable parts of a whole, each part flowing into the other as foot merges into ankle or thighs into torso, losing separate identity (Figure 31).

Potters in India and Southeast Asia have a beautiful method for making jars. The clay is first thrown on the wheel but only the neck and the lip are given final form. The clay below is left very thick and the volume of the jar is less than half that of the piece when finished. The wall of this unfinished part below may be about half-an-inch thick or more. The unfinished piece is cut off the wheel and drying is begun. The neck and lip, being finished and quite thin, naturally dry more rapidly than the part below and reach stiffness while the bottom part is still quite soft. When drying has reached the right stage, the potter begins to expand the body of the jar by paddling. He holds a rounded piece of wood on the inside and beats with a paddle on the outside. These tools are frequently dusted with dry clay to keep them from sticking to the pot. The pot is rhythmically pounded over its whole surface, the potter continuously shifting his tools to a new spot. As he pounds the pot grows outward into a rounded form. Sometimes the paddle used on the outside is carved with an incised design which gives a texture to the surface

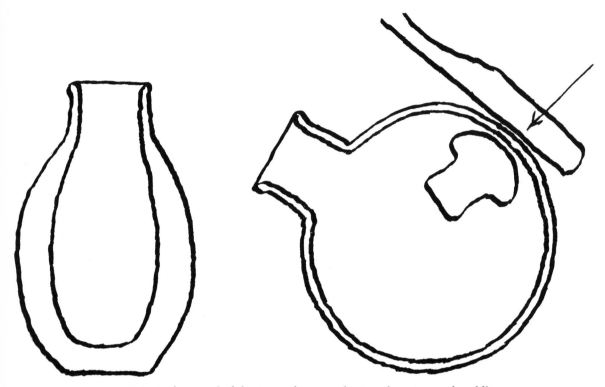

Fig. 34   Indian method for jar-making, combining throwing and paddling.

of the clay. From the description it would seem that this would be a long and laborious process, but actually a potter can finish one piece this way in about five or six minutes (Fig. 34). Jars made with this "hammer and anvil" technique have a different quality of form from thrown pieces. The surface is very smooth and even, and the general shape tends to be globular, without the progression of shape from bottom upward. But the interior space is strongly felt.

10 BOTTLES

Jars have been used for a wide variety of contents such as liquids, grains, pickles, tea, seeds, foods of all kinds, granola, rose petals, or the ashes of the dead. Bottles are more specifically intended to hold liquids and to protect them from evaporation or spillage. Jars tend towards massiveness and strength; bottles are more often small, delicate, and refined in shape. The elements of the form which make up the bottle, a voluminous body surmounted by a small neck or opening, create a dynamism or tension more pronounced than the more relaxed proportions of the jar or vase.

WORKING THE BOTTLE

On the wheel, the body of the bottle must be completed before the radical collaring in at the top begins (Figure 15). Thus, some planning is required in the shaping of the lower part, since it is no longer accessible for adjustments from the inside after the neck is brought in. Too often the body of the bottle, after the neck is formed, is found to be meager or timid in shape. Here the profile stick is very useful. After the neck has been narrowed to the point where the hand will not pass, the stick can be used to swell out the form further and to adjust its curve. The use of the stick for this purpose requires a delicacy of touch, because the movement and give of the clay is felt only through the tool and not the fingers. The wider the body of the bottle and the more boldly stated the curve of its shoulder, the more difficulty will be encountered in successfully bringing in the neck and finishing it without collapse.

One method of bottle-making which permits greater extremes of form is to throw only the bottom part of the piece first, up to and a little beyond the shoulder. The clay is then allowed to dry until it has stiffened a bit, perhaps for an hour or two under normal drying conditions. Then a fat coil or doughnut of clay is added at the top (Figure 35). This coil is carefully brought on center and the neck is formed from it, alternating between thinning and collaring in. The advantage of this approach is that it gives more freedom in the shaping of the body of the bottle since it need not withstand the strain of the inward construction. Also, the neck can be made as long as desired without having to reserve clay for it at the top of the thrown form.

The bottle, being an almost closed-in form, has a feeling of mass and volume (Figure 41). Communication with the inside is minimal. But the inside may be strongly felt, nevertheless, as a distension, a pressure from within. Slackness or looseness of form seems more inappropriate in bottles than it does in the more open pottery forms. Permutations of the bottle form are endless. They may be globular, teardropped, double-bellied, cylindrical. The bottle is a relatively complete form, not waiting to be completed by its content. We feel that bottles can stand on their own and owe little to function to be appreciated. The rounded, compact form of the bottle with perhaps an almost flat shoulder area, presents an ideal surface for the display of glaze, and potters whose interest centers on richly colored or textured glazes often use the bottle as their principal form. Light falls on the shoulder of the bottle, bringing out its form and color; unlike a bowl which absorbs light into its interior, its sides remaining somewhat shadowed.

BREATHING INTO A CLAY FORM

Though sometimes done as a trick, blowing up a freshly made bottle with the breath demonstrates some things about the shape. You place your mouth on the neck of the bottle (a little clay in the mouth won't hurt) and blow gently. The soft clay of the bottle gives under the pressure of the air and expands lightly like a balloon. This stretching and extension can sometimes make a perfunctory form miraculously come alive. Pressure from within supplies what may have been lacking before, a sense of the inside, a positive feeling of interior space. Flat places in the form are blown out and the curves of the profile are unified and brought together. One could anticipate that the

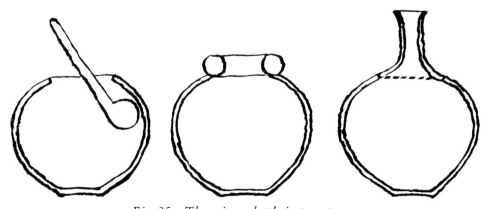

Fig. 35   Throwing a bottle in two stages.

end result of this blowing might approach a perfect sphere. The sphere is said to be the most difficult of all forms to throw, but even when achieved it proves to be a form in which the dynamics of growth and change have resulted in static perfection.

WORKING A CLOSED-IN FORM

Another manipulation sometimes used in demonstrations of throwing is closing in the bottle form entirely and then working on the resulting shape, which is like a blown-up balloon. To do this, the neck is narrowed as usual, then finally closed off altogether. This traps the air inside and gives an amazing resistance and springiness to the form; it can be raised or pushed down into a lower shape without collapsing. Forms which would be very difficult to achieve any other way can be done with this technique. The air inside can be felt as a palpable force which, beyond a certain point, resists any radical change from the spherical. If one wishes to finish a piece done this way, the clay can be allowed to dry until stiffened, then a new opening is cut in the top and a neck added as described above.

Bottles tend towards the nonfunctional since the actual job of containing liquids has pretty much been taken over by metals, glass, and plastic. The opacity of pottery makes it inferior to glass if the visibility of the contents is important. I feel that pottery bottles are not quite right for wine. The color of the wine is obscured and there is no way to tell how much is left in the bottle. Sake, as served in Japan, is best in a ceramic bottle because it must be warmed and kept warm for serving. Because glass was rare, in ancient times pottery bottles were used for wine and for oils. But the absorbency of the soft unglazed pottery bodies must have created problems of seepage and spoiling. Pharmacy was greatly advanced with the advent of ceramic glazes because bottles and jars for drugs in liquid form and for the various oils and essences could then be made relatively impervious and nonporous.

The profile of a bottle is sometimes seen stamped on clay or used in advertisements as a symbol of pottery-making. Useful or not, the bottle has stayed in the potter's repertoire (Figures 36 through 40, 42 and 43).

Fig. 36   Overleaf. *Bottle. A rising, swelling form is terminated by a collared opening.*
Fig. 37   Overleaf, left to right. *Bottle. The melon-shaped body supports a small neck.*
Fig. 38   *Bottle. The sinuous profile leads upward, terminating in the slightly spreading neck.*
Fig. 39   *Bottle. The teardrop shape expresses the function of the bottle.*
Fig. 40   *Bottle. The body is a flattened oval, giving broad-based stability.*

11 TRIMMING & FEET

Trimming means shaving or paring off the clay from a thrown form. This operation is done on the leather hard clay. It can define and sharpen the form, get rid of excessive thickness, and produce various textures.

TOOLS

Tools for trimming are shown in Figure 45. A hooked knife can be made by bending the flexible type of potter's knife. It cuts well, but cuts only one kind of groove. The "pear corer" was actually designed for cutting out the core from pears but has become a standard trimming tool. The varied contour of the tool permits cuts of various sorts. It is a very good tool. The hooked tool works well but is limited in the cuts it can make. Loop tools are also very efficient for shaving off clay but limited as to cut. Japanese type trimming tools are made in a variety of profiles from flexible steel. The bamboo tool is good for shaving off the side of a pot but not for forming a cut shape such as a foot.

TRIMMING METHODS

If the objective of trimming is to shave down the wall of the pot and to make it a bit thinner toward the bottom, the pot can be centered on the wheel right side up. The pot must be dry enough to handle easily but not stiff. The pot is carefully centered on the wheel head, then a few drops of water are run under it with a syringe. With a little pressing it will stick to the wheel head. Trimming then proceeds with the wheel running at a fairly brisk speed. If the clay comes off in flakes the pot is too dry. If the clay balls up on the trimming tool it is too wet. When the dryness of the pot is just right, the

Fig. 41 Opposite, left to right. *Bottle. The cylindrical form of the middle zone is played against the domes of the bottom and the top.*
Fig. 42 *Bottle. The body is almost spherical, surmounted by a neck and collar.*
Fig. 43 *Bottle. The neck grows out of the body in one sweeping curve.*
Fig. 44 *Knees.*

55

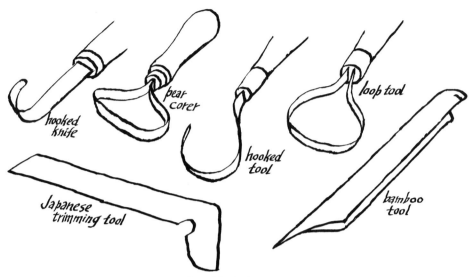

Fig. 45   Tools for trimming.

trimmings come off in long, unbroken ribbons. Only a little is shaved off at a time. The wheel is stopped occasionally for a test of thickness. If the clay gives to the pressure of the finger, the right thickness of wall is probably being approached. Tapping while listening to the tone produced will also indicate the relative thickness, the lower the tone the thicker the wall. When an open jar or bowl is being trimmed a needle or wire may be run through the wall from the outside until it is felt by the finger inside, thus measuring the actual thickness of the wall.

If clay is to be trimmed off the bottom of the pot or if a foot ring is to be cut, the pot is centered upside down on the wheel. To do this, one must be sure that the pot is stiff enough so it can be handled and set on its rim without distortion.

CENTERING METHODS

To center, the piece may be carefully placed within the nearest fitting concentric circle on the metal wheel head or circle drawn on the wooden or plaster wheel head with a pencil. Off-centeredness can be detected by holding a pencil or needle point against the side of the slowing revolving pot. Another way to center a piece for trimming is by bumping or tapping. The pot is placed on the smooth wheel head, and with the wheel going slowly it is tapped or bumped with the right hand, the left hand being used as a guide, until it finds center.

Tapping on center is a skill which is not easily acquired. No one can teach you to do it, because the adepts themselves do not know exactly how it works. The first tap, or the first ten for that matter, may only make the pot travel more eccentrically. But eventually one tap or a series of taps put the pot on perfect center. One theory of tapping is that the eye is fixed on the side of the pot opposite to the one being tapped and when the bulge of off-center comes to that point the hand taps. The slowness of this reaction assures that the tap will actually be delivered to the pot when the bulge has travelled around a half revolution to where the tapping hand is. The trouble with this theory is that good pot-bumpers hardly seem to look at the pot. It is uncanny that a pot can be centered in this manner with no more than two or three bumps. Perhaps it signifies that the potter has achieved maturity in centering, the ability to feel for center and to find it without searching. The best pot-bumpers are the decorators in the dinnerware factories who daily center hundreds of plates on the banding wheel prior to applying color bands with the brush. One, or, at most, two taps and the plate runs perfectly true. Mold shop craftsmen also have great skill in centering. They are able to center large plaster case molds on the wheel head, using only a few slaps with the palm of the hand.

The inverted and centered pot is fastened to the wheel head with three or four wads of clay. In the case of pots with long necks or very narrow openings, a chum must be used to hold the piece for trimming (Figure 46). The pot then rests securely on its shoulder rather than on the fragile lip. Chums may be made on the wheel in various sizes and shapes and given a bisque fire for permanence. Or a special chum may be made to hold a particular piece and used in the leather hard state. A chuck (Figure 46) is a hump used to hold bowls for trimming. Chucks are useful when a number of bowls of almost identical size and shape are to be trimmed. The bowls are lightly pushed down on the chuck and quickly come onto center.

Before turning a pot upside down to trim, the inside shape is studied carefully and some decision made as to the shaping of the bottom or the design of the foot. If the inside of the piece is not sensed during trimming there is a danger that the inside and the outside will not relate well to each other. The trimming should be thought of as a completion of the clay membrane which holds the hollow, rather than a tooling down of something solid.

The relative softness or hardness of the clay is important. If a soft, plastic feeling is desired, the trimming is done on quite soft clay, with a slow turning wheel and bold cutting with the tool. Smooth or precise forms are trimmed from harder clay with a rapidly turning wheel and small, sharp tools.

It will be noted that tooling the clay on an inverted pot, if the cutting proceeds from foot toward lip, will produce spiral grooves going in the opposite direction to the grooves produced by the fingers on the thrown surface. This can give a feeling of confrontation where the two kinds of grooves meet. To avoid this, the pot can be trimmed in motions which start on the wall and work upwards toward the foot.

To trim an inverted pot, the bottom is usually leveled off first, starting at the edge and working toward the center. At first the problem is to get rid of the eccentricities which are sure to be present no matter how carefully the pot was thrown and centered. Then the bottom is shaved off until it is judged to be the proper thickness. When the proper thickness for the bottom has been reached, a slight flexibility or give in the clay can be felt. Thickness can also be gauged by tapping with the finger and noting the tone produced. If the tone is lower than that given by the upper, thrown part of the pot, it means that the cross section is thicker. Next, the sides are trimmed and the final shape given to the bottom. If no foot ring is made, the bottom is usually dented in somewhat. The reason for doing this is that a pot with a flat bottom teeters if the slightest crumb is under it, whereas a piece with a concave bottom will teeter only if a crumb is under the circular area which actually touches the table. Attention to all of these petty details can contribute to usefulness, if not to beauty.

Some potters working for speed like to trim pieces without fastening them down to the head. Light pieces are kept on center by holding the left palm against the spinning pot. Heavier pieces seem to stay put quite well just from gravity. But there is a chance that the pot will be hooked by the tool and fly off the wheel.

There are purists who do not approve of shaving down pots. They feel that this is an admission of failure because the skillful thrower is theoretically ca-

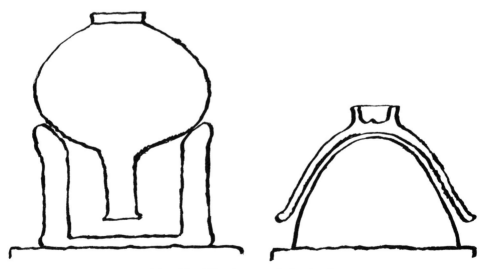

Fig. 46   The chum and the chuck.

pable of making pots of almost any shape which are of just the right thickness as they come from the wheel. Some also feel that trimming, since it removes the fingermarks which are the hallmarks of throwing, destroys some of the direct relationship between process, form and surface. But most potters follow a practical course, and trim whenever it is necessary to thin the clay to the proper weight. Pots are often too thick toward the bottom, especially in the case of large or difficult forms, and it is beneficial for the form if some of this extra clay is taken off. Anyway the throwing marks which count in design are usually at midsection or higher, where trimming is unnecessary. It is true that pots which are trimmed too much may take on the look of turned wood rather than clay, and attempts to simulate throwing marks with the shaving tool are usually not entirely successful.

It may be difficult to make the quality of the trimmed part of a pot sympathetic to the more plastic nature of the part which was thrown. The trimmed part can become hard, dry, and mechanical, rather the opposite of those aspects of thrown clay which may be valued most such as fluidity, spontaneity, movement, and integral texture. There are no rules for solving this problem, but it is helpful to keep trimming to a minimum and to maintain a feeling of plasticity in the trimmed part by running the wheel more slowly, using sharp tools, and working on clay which is not too hard. Successful trimming is a matter of being respectful of the clay and of the quality existing in the thrown part. The trimming is a kind of obbligato; it is subsidiary, complementary, and possibly harmonious with the rest. Trimmed surfaces are a little gritty compared to the fingered parts. There is more sharpness of edge and plane. Rather than being rounded and smooth, the trimmed part can be textured and angular, crisp rather than soft. The quality is that of something which has been cut rather than squeezed into final shape. The union of the trimmed with the thrown seems to take care of itself when the conditions are right; it is a matter of tools, consistency of clay, speed of wheel, and touch. It all comes down to touch in the end.

WEIGHT

Pottery is highly tactile; the feel of a pot is an important aspect of its character. Thus the weight of a pot becomes important. Weight is part of the tactile sensation of picking up a pot and handling it. Thinness and lightness are equated with delicacy, attenuation, and fragility. Thickness and heaviness connect with inertia, rootedness, immobility, and the solid as against the hollow. Somewhere between these extremes, each pot seems to have its proper weight. Because of the difficulty of thinning out the walls when throwing, especially around the base, the beginner experiences a long struggle with overweight. His pots may look quite well from the outside, but their heaviness reveals that there is an incongruity between inside and outside. The problem is more than just a matter of thickness. If the walls of a pot are too thick they do not respond to the touch during the making process and tend toward stiffness and inflexibility. The walls of the pot need to move and to breathe during creation. The whole value of throwing as a process may be negated if the pot remains too thick to move easily under the pressure of the fingers.

FEET

In cultures where pottery was made by hand, feet were uncommon. The base of the majority of hand built pots is simply a rounded bottom or a bottom with a concavity. It is possible that when glazes came into use, the foot ring was developed as a device for preventing the glazed pieces from sticking to their saggers or supports. The early glazes developed in Egypt and the Middle East often ran badly in the fire. With a foot ring, the pot could be glazed all over except for the bottom of the ring, and set up on little wads of clay so the fluid glaze would run off and not stick the pot to the surface it was sitting on. Trimmed feet appear on some of the earliest thrown pottery of China, dating back to at least 1000 B.C. In China, however, the higher fired and more stable glazes made the foot relatively unnecessary as far as control of glaze run goes. Nevertheless, the foot became an important feature of almost all Chinese pots. The foot enabled the potters to more easily stack one piece on another in the kiln without sticking. In the finished pottery, feet enabled bowls and plates to be stacked neatly and with less danger of breakage and thus facilitating packing and shipment. On rice bowls and tea bowls, the foot made the pieces much more easy to pick up, to pass, and to hold in the hands.

I have been making feet on pots and studying the design of feet for many years, but I still find them interesting and a challenge to do properly. This obsession with feet, this "foot fetish" would be hard to explain to a non-potter. Potters all seem to have a keen interest in what goes on at the bottom of the piece.

When a foot ring is to be cut, the pot is thrown with some extra clay left at the bottom. It is better to leave an ample amount as this will give more freedom in decisions about height and shape. The bottom of the pot is leveled off with the tool first. Then the ring is cut, usually making the hollow inside of the ring first and probing for the actual bottom surface. The form of the foot emerges as the cutting proceeds. In the case of a small bowl, the whole trimming process may not take more than a minute or two. The diameter of the foot and the shape of the bottom are made with reference to the inside form.

The foot, rather than being cut from excess clay at the bottom, may be made by adding clay. This is usually done when a high foot or stem is de-

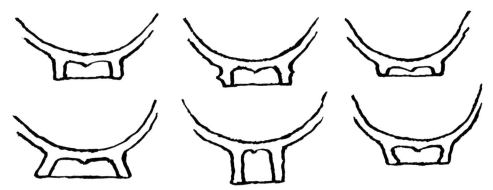

Fig. 47   Various foot-ring forms.

sired. In this method, the bottom of the piece is trimmed off and thinned, without a foot. Then a coil or doughnut of plastic clay is fastened to the bottom of the piece with slip (Figure 48). It is laid down in as circular a shape as possible, then centered. This fresh clay is then thrown and shaped into a foot; irregularities are cut off with a needle. The advantage of this method is that any size or height of foot can be made without having to reserve a mass of clay at the bottom when throwing. Another advantage may be that the foot, being shaped wet from plastic clay, grows naturally out of the rest of the pot. High feet or stems can be made on goblets or compotes using this technique. Or such feet can be thrown separately and fastened on in the leather hard state.

A high foot usually has no specific function. But it may give a feeling of dignity to a form, lifting it off the ground plane and making it easier to see and to approach. The same effect, entirely psychological, can be observed in the change that seems to come about in a sculpture when it is placed on a pedestal or base. This effect is exemplified by the pots shown in Figures 154 and 169.

The foot stands as a kind of trademark or signature of the potter. Subtle differences in style, method, and emphasis will distinguish the maker's approach. The actual stamped or brushed signature will usually appear within the foot ring. Far from being an unimportant detail of the pot, the foot contributes greatly to a sense of stability, or origin. Visually, the foot seems to give the pot a lift or spring from its base. It alleviates that dumpiness often felt in pots which rest directly on their bottoms. The foot allows a little air to circulate toward the bottom and the pot breathes more easily. Light can penetrate and lift the form from below. The first stirring of the curves of the profile will be felt at the base just above the foot.

The foot can be shaped in many ways (Fig. 47). It can be cylindrical, or it may splay slightly inward or outward. If the foot is to belong to the pot, its scale and shape must be made with reference to the whole. It is my observation that most beginners cut feet on pots which seem too wide in diameter and too thick. The opposite tendency, feet which are tiny and delicate can also be very out of place on certain forms. Following the "middle way" in this as in the other traditional approaches to the design of the details of pottery can help one avoid, perhaps, grossly incongruous parts. But the real life of a pot always seems to arise from something other than the application of such rules.

Since the foot is often bare of glaze, at least on its lower surface, the naked clay is displayed and contrasted with the smooth surface of the glaze. Dark against light, rough against smooth, cut against thrown, earthy against glassy; from these opposites the foot makes its contribution to the form.

POTTER'S MARKS

Although it might be considered a minor detail, the mark or signature on the bottom of a pot can contribute to the distinction of the design. Signatures which are stamped or scratched into the damp clay seem more authentic than those which are painted on the body with stains or which appear under or on the glaze. The stamped mark being in the clay itself signifies that it was done during the actual birth of the pot. I am in favor of signing pots, and I believe that the signature should be legible. Much of the history of European pottery and porcelain has been unraveled by the study of potters' marks. The signature serves as more than an identification; it is also a gesture of affirmation by the potter saying, in effect, "This, for better or for worse, is *my* work."

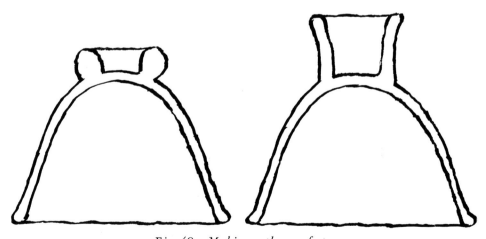

Fig. 48 Making a thrown foot.

12 THROWING OFF THE HUMP & DUPLICATE FORMS

THROWING OFF THE HUMP

Rather than centering a ball of clay for each piece to be made, pots may be made from the top part of a larger lump of clay centered on the wheel. The clay, usually a piece weighing ten pounds or more, is centered and drawn up into a somewhat conical shape. At the top of the cone, a section is isolated from the rest by squeezing at the sides with the fingers, cutting a groove. This upper section is then shaped into a hemisphere just as is done in centering an individual ball of clay. Throwing then proceeds as usual. When the pot is finished, a rather deep groove is cut under it with the stick. It is possible to cut this groove at exactly the right level to mark the finished bottom of the pot. Or, if the piece is to have a trimmed foot, excess clay may be allowed. Then, with the wheel running at slow speed, one end of a cord is caught in the groove. The cord is carried around and when it has encircled about three-fourths of the diameter it is pulled, cutting the pot free from the hump. The piece is then picked up in the usual way. Another method of cutting small pieces off the hump is to use a broad steel spatula, well moistened. This is held horizontally and gradually edged into the groove. At a certain point the pot is cut away and released from the hump, skidding over onto the spatula.

Throwing off the hump, since it eliminates the time required for individually centering each piece, can be fast. It is a good method for doing relaxation exercises on the wheel. My favorite exercise for overcoming tightness, stiffness, over-precision or over-design is to throw quickly a series of very small pots off the hump. Only a moment is devoted to each piece, making accuracy or planning ahead impossible. Each small piece, whether a plate, bowl, or cup, springs up between the fingers in a few seconds and is immediately cut off. In this exercise the potter should work mostly by feel, hardly looking at the work. A whole group of little pots appear on the ware board, each with its distinctive form and each having sprung into being without plan. It is like being the instrument of creation!

Pottery Form

DUPLICATE FORMS

The beginner faces what seems like a never-ending struggle with the wayward clay. Just to get it to rise up from the wheel head and become a reasonably precise cylinder taxes all his skill. The idea of making two pieces which are alike may seem preposterously difficult. But it is possible. Even in the first stages of learning to throw it is very helpful to work with balls of clay of the same weight and to try to make pairs or quintuplets. (Several methods for checking the accuracy and similarity of forms of identical size are illustrated in Figure 49).

Aside from being a training exercise, what is the place of duplicated forms in the art of pottery? When several or many pieces are made which are more or less alike, it may seem like a contradiction of the most important objective of wheel work, usually considered to be the generation of fresh, original forms and the exploration of their possibilities. Unrelieved repetition of anything can become boring, deadening. One of the main reservations which those who practice the arts of painting and sculpture have about the crafts and about pottery in particular is that if the work is repetitious and the end result thoroughly foreseen before the work begins, there can be no creativity, no art. After all, the distinction between the artist and the craftsman is often thought to be that the craftsman merely executes an established design while an artist creates a new one. Can a mold-made piece of pottery which has 200 replicas be a work of art? Can a mold-made piece of pottery which has no replicas be a work of art? If a Rodin sculpture exists in four identical bronze versions, are they all works of art? If so, what is the difference between this replication and that of the craftsman who makes four beautiful pitchers, all more or less alike? If there are answers to these questions, I do not know them.

Pottery-making in most cultures has usually involved an ongoing production of countless pieces, all fitting within more or less well-established designs or types. If that were not so, if each potter had followed his own whims while working, archeologists would not be able to use the remains of pottery as a means of dating and separating various cultures and subcultures. Etruscan pottery, for example, has its own repertoire of shapes and styles, and although they are similar to some Greek pottery, Etruscan work can be easily distinguished from anything Greek. Similarly, Korean pottery, in a way a kind of an offshoot of Chinese ceramics, is distinctive in form and decoration and has quite a different feel from anything Chinese. These distinct styles or types of pottery came about through a long development during which certain forms were perfected and stabilized through repetition.

The question is how, in the past, were deadness, dullness, and deterioration of forms avoided in repetitive work? The answer seems to be that in the

64

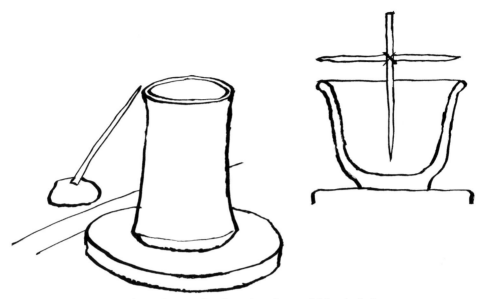

Fig. 49   Gauges for throwing forms of identical size.

past, when craftsmanship was the source of all useful or ceremonial artifacts, craftsmen became involved in their work as whole men rather than as disinterested hired hands or mechanics. That is, they did not withhold themselves in the practice of their craft. Their impulses, their *joie de vivre,* their strength, their poise, their breathing, their feeling got into the work. Thus each piece which they made emerged as a new object with energy and vitality infused into it, even though it may have been almost identical in form to a previously made example. Their work could be compared to the concert artist of today who creates, say, a Beethoven sonata each time he plays it. It floats out into the air as if for the first time, even though the artist may have played the same piece the day before. We must remember also that in past cultures in which craftsmanship was the principal means of production, all of the artifacts produced had this same quality of vigor and rightness. Clothing, pottery, tools, musical instruments, and houses were individually created works.

I hope I am not romanticizing the working habits of our forebears. Lots of humdrum pots were made in the past and repetitive work in many places and times no doubt sapped rather than nurtured creativity. The point is that repetition under certain conditions does not necessarily preclude lively, meaningful forms.

For us, the repetition of a shape, making a whole boardful of pitchers or mugs which are much alike, may have an association with mass production or factory work. We can become tired of the work and our attention may wander from it. The design of a repeated piece may gradually change until it too takes on a tired look. Quantity can endanger quality. If, in order to save labor, the craftsman decides to use molds and the jigger wheel, he may end up operating a factory, even if it has only one employee, himself. If the potter is interested primarily in pots, rather than the financial rewards which might follow on their making, he needs to adopt an attitude toward repeated shapes which will generate interest and energy rather than dissipate it.

While repetitious work has its dangers for potters as they define themselves today, the evolution or development of a form through multiple examples unquestionably has the potential of reaching deep levels of integrity within the pot. In pottery, as in other endeavors, the first try is not usually the most successful. The forms we make tend to mellow and to ripen as our identification with them grows. When a form is perfected over a series of examples, it acquires a sureness, clarity, and directness which may be missing in a pot made as a single, unique example. What we call style, or the flavor which distinguishes one person's work from another, seldom results from some mental calculation. Rather, it grows out of the work itself. Interest in a certain kind of form can lead one to explore that form and to probe its mysteries fully. The growth of the form, as it changes and finds expression in successive examples, can be like the growth of the person. The child may be a complete and beautiful person, but he is also a bundle of potentialities. The nature of these potentialities cannot be known until they unfurl with time. Although we retain the same social security number through life, what we are tomorrow is not what we were yesterday. We ourselves are "multiple examples" developed and ripened by experience.

13 BOWLS

The basic, primal forms of pottery are the jar and the bowl. The jar tends to be massive, contained, sculptural, centered, isolated. It grasps its interior space firmly, defines it and holds it. The bowl is open, wide-mouthed, exposed, vulnerable. It holds its space lightly, because its interior is really part of the surrounding space, and is connected and flowing into it. The closed-in forms of pottery bring to mind pods, roots, vegetables, eggs, or marine shells. The bowl suggests rather an open blossom or the two cupped hands. According to Greek myth, the first bowl was shaped over the breast of Aphrodite.

The form of the bowl offers relatively little scope for sculptural complexity. Its simple shape, basically a hollow hemisphere or variations on the hemisphere, can be expressed with many subtle variations and nuances, but it can hardly yield drama or that anthropomorphism which brings vitality to many upright pottery forms. The bowl is basically a modest form. As a shape it is unobtrusive, quiet, low, restrained. In his bowls, the individuality of the potter speaks in whispers. But whispers can be as expressive as shouts.

Since the bowl is an open form which we look down into, its interior becomes an encircled and defined area. Our attention is thus concentrated on the color, texture, and substance of the clay and the glaze, as well as the design or decoration on the interior. It is like the dome of the sky. We project into it as open space but feel the definition of the horizon. The decoration on the inside of a bowl is entirely different in field from the decoration appearing on the outside of a closed-in form such as a jar. On the jar, the decoration circles the outside in an endless continuum, but in the bowl the design is held in the fixed realm of the circle. If the bowl is decorated on both the inside and the outside, these two still remain separated by the rim and are experienced differently.

Making a bowl on the wheel may seem easy compared to raising a cylinder. The clay is encouraged in its natural tendency to flare outward into a low form. But a complete resolution of the form—the bringing together of the lip, the profile, the interior volume, and the foot—will be found to be very elusive, a challenging problem in fact. Why do some bowls seem to have a sense of music about them, an authentic posture and grace, while others are mere dishes?

After the centered ball is hollowed out, the rudimentary cylinder is formed and allowed to spread outward into something approaching a cone shape (Figure 53). This cone is kept more upright than the intended final bowl. As thinning proceeds, the walls of the bowl are not encouraged to develop any curve because as soon as the profile curves, further thinning can lead to slumping. The width of the base is important. If it is too narrow, the chance of slumping is increased; if it is too wide, the lower part of the bowl can be shaped only from the inside and not the outside, which leads to stiffness and lack of response in the form.

The bowl is given its final shape in the last few pulls. Each pull starts from the very center and ends with the steadying of the rim by the fingers (Figure 60).

FORM

The form of the bowl is actually established by the pressure from the left hand, which swells the shape outward. The form can be totally felt from the inside, but visual examination of the outside curve may suggest changes, development or exaggeration. A rounded rib is sometimes useful in shaping the inside, but too much reliance on the rib can result in a mechanical shape which merely reflects the established shape of the rib rather than the inspired urgings of the fingers.

A difficulty often occurs at the point where the clay moves out and away from the supporting base underneath. A kind of shelf can develop here caused by the slump of the bowl at the point where it reaches beyond the

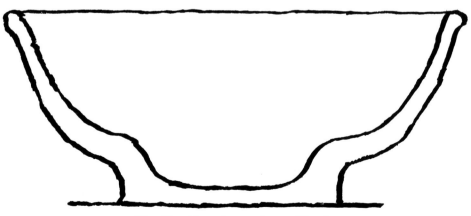

Fig. 50 Slumping tendency of bowls.

support of the thicker clay below (Figure 50). This unwanted shelf can be avoided by controlling the thickness of the piece and by starting each pull from the center.

DRYING

Drying is more critical in open bowls than it is with the more enclosed forms. As the bowl dries, the walls shrink and rise inward, giving a higher form with a smaller diameter than the original contour. What seems a very low bowl when freshly thrown will usually turn out to be much higher when dry. To compensate for this tendency, the bowl can be made flatter than desired at first, with allowance made for the upwards shrinkage. Or, the bowl can be put back on the wheel and flattened down again after it has dried somewhat, working with the rib or the fingers. As soon as possible, bowls should be cut off their bats and inverted on a smooth flat surface so they may dry evenly. Drying stresses show up later as cracks or distortions in the fired piece.

TRIMMING

Since bowls are made quite thick at the bottom to keep them from slumping downward, they usually require trimming. Trimming establishes a form at the bottom which faithfully responds to the shape of the inside of the bowl. The foot may be cut from the extra clay or added onto the trimmed surface using a coil of fresh clay (Figure 47).

The features of the bowl are few, but relating them into a coherent whole can involve a considerable study. The surface of the inside is usually made smooth for easy cleaning and to give little friction or obstruction to the action of spoons or other serving or mixing tools. The action of throwing may leave a perfect spiral originating in the exact center and moving outward toward the rim. This can be left, and if the finger marks are shallow the surface will be smoothed out with the covering of glaze.

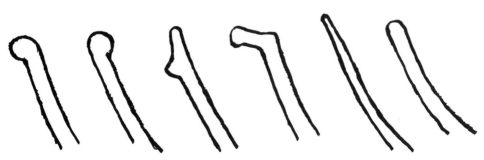

Fig. 51   Lips.

Fig. 52 Bowl. The outward and upward movement of the form are balanced and about equal. Foot and body are integrated.

THE BOWL LIP

The lip of the bowl is often made with a slight thickening or bead (Figure 60). This helps to prevent warping and has a reinforcing effect. The lip of the bowl is the part we see and touch first, and it tells much of the style and spirit of the potting. It may be thick and rugged, or paper thin and delicate. It may turn slightly inward, or outward. It may be thin right at the lip itself but show a thickening just below that. Or, a small flat form may be made resembling the rim of a plate. Any turn of the lip or thickening at the edge will make the bowl easier to pick up and to handle (Figure 51).

THE BOWL PROFILE

The profile or curve can be made in many ways, each having its own subtle influence on the presence of the bowl. The curve may be essentially a segment of a circle, giving the bowl the form of a hemisphere (Figure 57). However, a curve derived from a circle seems to lack dynamism, and it may give a mechanical appearance. A curve based on the parabola is more active since it continuously changes and flattens out toward a straight line (Figure 59). Turning the lip of the bowl outward produces an S curve from foot to lip. If the two ends of this S curve are similar, a rather static quality results. A more dynamic and moving profile is achieved when the two ends of the S are different (Figures 54 and 61). Of course, these prescriptions about the profile must be taken with a grain of salt; they hardly hold as rules. But if the bowl is studied with reference to the kinds of profiles it displays, a better understanding may be gained of its essential form. There is also the possibility of combining straight and curvilinear elements in the profile. This results in a break or change of direction and can enhance the sense of structure and proportion (Figures 55 and 62).

The bowl may be controlled, precisely formed, and "tense," or it may be loosely put together and relaxed. The Chinese potters of the Sung period were masters of bowl making, and the stoneware and porcelain pieces they made are somehow "more than the sum of the parts." Old Chinese bowls tend to be carefully formed and show a strict harmony between rim, profile, and foot. Korean and Japanese bowls tend to be more casual and often have forms and textures which suggest rapid and rhythmical forming, with more of the mark of the finger and tool surviving in the finished work.

Fig. 53 Overleaf left, top. *Starting a bowl. Even in this early stage, the clay is made to stretch outward into the beginnings of a bowl shape.*
Fig. 54 Overleaf left, bottom. *Bowl. Although the form is nearly straight-sided, the profile curve maintains a continuous dynamic from foot to lip.*
Fig. 55 Overleaf right. *Bowl. Similar to the bowl in Figure 54, but here the sides come closer to a straight line profile. The foot is trimmed as an articulated part.*

Fig. 56   Bowl. The form stretches out from the foot but then turns inward, giving a feeling of enclosed space.

Fig. 57   Bowl. Essentially a hemisphere, the form is accentuated and terminated by a slight outward turn at the lip.

Fig. 58   Bowl. The form suggests a gentle opening up or widening to the sky.

Fig. 59   Bowl. The profile is close to a parabolic curve. However, the lip is turned slightly outward. The foot blends into the bowl form.

Fig. 60   Throwing a bowl. The fingers gather on the lip to smooth and shape it.

CROSS SECTIONS

Unlike the more closed-in pottery forms such as vases and bottles, the bowl has a cross section which can be reached, felt, and gauged by the fingers. The subtle thinning of the cross section from foot to lip, and the thickening of the lip establish the feel of the bowl. The clumsily made bowl often shows inconsistencies in cross section such as excessive thickness near the base or thin places where the trimming went too far. The bowl may be very thin and have an eggshell quality, or it may be given a substantial and sturdy substance. Or the form can be distorted by gentle squeezing before the clay has begun to stiffen.

FEET

Bowls may be made without feet; they can have just simple rounded bottoms. But the tooled or added foot is a traditional feature of the bowl and adds importantly to its distinction. It makes the piece easier to pick up by raising the form slightly. With a foot, the rounding of the form on the underneath is more visible. The foot can be thought of as an added form, with the curve of the bowl having a continuous sweep through the bottom. Or the foot can grow out of the form with no distinct articulation (Figures 54 and 63).

If the foot is made too narrow, the bowl will be unstable, and practicality will have been sacrificed to elegance and poise. If the foot is too wide, the bowl may appear bottom heavy, earthbound, and lacking in "spring." The beginner usually errs on the side of making the foot too wide. The beginner also tends to cut the foot ring without reference to the scale and cross section of the rest of the piece, and may end up with a foot which is much thicker or much thinner than the substance of the rest of the bowl.

The quality of translucence is at its best in bowl forms. In thin porcelains the interior can hold the light and pass it mysteriously to the outside. Thickness or thinness can modify this light. The Chinese "rice design" on bowls is actually done by perforating the bowl with numerous small oblong holes, which fill in with glaze. These look like grains of translucent rice imbedded in the body. The Persians also used perforations filled with glaze to produce patterns of light.

Fig. 61 Bowl. This is the "rice bowl" type. The profile is a rather taut S curve. The trimmed foot is wide enough for stability but narrow enough so as not to interrupt the sweep of the bottom.

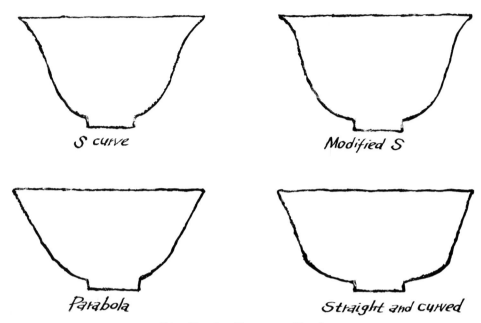

Fig. 62   Profile curves of bowls.

Glazes tend to run downward and may leave the lip of the bowl thinly glazed. This slipping away of the glaze from the edge may result in an accent of a differing shade than the rest of the glaze. Glaze may also tend to gather near the foot in a thickened roll or in droplets. On the inside, the glaze runs toward the bottom surface, often creating a pool or puddle of glaze. These events, controlled or accidental, accentuate the form.

Bowls have a rather generalized function. Empty, they hold air nicely. The interior is open, ready to receive or to give out. As a container for food and offerings, the form of the bowl has attained a universal nature. It will never be obsolete. Shaped like a bell, the well-fired bowl gives a rich, lingering, musical note, and this ring can be thought of as the symbol of the transformation of the formless clay dust into its fired structure of permanence, hardness, and density. (In India there is a musical instrument, the *jaltarang*, which is made up of porcelain cups of various sizes, struck like a xylophone.)

If one were to be reduced to one possession only, besides clothing, it might be a bowl. Buddhist monks in fact deny themselves all possessions except the begging bowl, which also doubles as a dish, washbasin, and drinking cup.

PLANTERS

Planters, made of earth, are meant to contain earth and its generative power. The planter is incomplete without its plant. As an incomplete form, it comes to life in use. The plant above takes dominance in the union of pot and container. But the quiet presence of the pot gives rootedness and place to the plant.

Plants literally love clay pots, and if it is true that plants can respond to stimuli with indications of pleasure and pain, plants rooted in ample, absorbent, thick-walled clay pots would signify their satisfaction with their pot. Plants in plastic, glass, metal, or wood would express various degrees of dissatisfaction. The absorbency of lightly fired clay benefits the growing plant by allowing it to breathe through its roots much as it would in loose soil. The permeable wall of the pot keeps the roots of the plant in touch with the world and not bound within a tight-walled prison. The absorbency of the pot permits it to hold and store moisture, and to release it back into the soil. Pot and soil are as one. If there is excess water, it is drained away not only through a drainage hole but by evaporation through the pot walls. The evaporative process decreases the temperature at the root, giving the plant the feeling of the cool earth below. Conversely, the high heat capacity of the pot slows down any sharp drop in temperature.

The humble red clay flower pot is an ideal planter, perfected over centuries of trading between horticulturists, nurserymen, and potters. The proportion is squarish, about as high as it is broad. The walls cant outward, making it easy to knock out the plant for replanting. The collar serves as reinforcement, as an aid to picking up, and as a shelf enabling the pots to be stacked one on the other in a straight column without the pots becoming wedged into each other. The drainage hole is big enough to prevent sogginess but does not allow earth to fall through. The saucer below catches the drainage, and stores some of the water for reabsorption up into the soil. This simple design has the beauty of perfect adaptation of form to function. As the pot is used, soluble salts from the soil seep out into the clay of the pot, depositing their solids on the outside as a whitish, grey, or greenish patina.

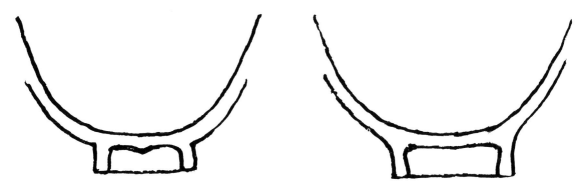

Fig. 63   Two ways of relating the foot to the bowl.

79

STONEWARE FOR PLANTERS

Planters made of stoneware have the virtue of durability, and may be used indoors on furniture or on the floor since they do not seep or leak. However, the advantages of porosity are lost to the plant, which might think it is in a metal can. No salty deposits appear on the outside of the pot, and some consider this an advantage.

The planter, then, is basically an open-mouthed pot, neither tall nor broad in form, opening out toward the lip, and providing drainage for the plant. It is potted rather thickly for strength and durability, and it sits on a broad and sturdy bottom to furnish a stable base for the plant above. It asserts itself only as an element in the sum *plant + pot.* A beautifully planted pot is a satisfying union of the natural with the man-made.

BULB BOWLS

Bulb bowls, meant to hold the bulbs in a stable situation without soil and in shallow water, are wide, low forms, broad enough to contain the desired number of bulbs. Drainage or absorbency is not required or desirable.

OTHER TYPES OF PLANTERS

The Bonsai dish is a specialized kind of planter. This form also is low and meant to contain only a relatively thin layer of soil. The walls turn outward to permit the easy removal of the plant. Provision for drainage must be ample, usually four or five holes. These holes are also used to anchor the wires which secure the roots, stabilizing the position of the plant. Saucers are not used because of the danger of waterlogged soil. Bonsai is usually thought of as a Japanese art, but it was and still is practiced in China. The Chinese term for Bonsai is *P'en-ching,* which means, literally, "pot-scapes," an indication of the importance given to the pot in the total concept of the art.

The art of flower arranging depends on pottery forms for containment and support. Many different kinds of pots may find a place in flower arrangement. In fact, the pottery container may be the starting point for an arrangement or, even, the dominant element in it.

The hanging planter, a pot suspended from above by three or more cords or ropes, is usually made of stoneware or glazed earthenware to prevent seepage. Drainage thus becomes a problem. Sometimes the hanging pot is made large enough so that a smaller absorbent pot can be placed inside it. The hanging planter is a rather unique pottery form because it is normally seen from below. Since the bottom of the planter is not only visible, but is the most prominent feature of the pot, its design can be developed in various ways—by texture, by the coming together of the elements of the form in a point or center, or by various decorative treatments of the clay.

14 PITCHERS

In the pitcher, the relationship of parts is clarified and logical. Body (1), neck (2), spout (3), and handle (4) are the subordinate parts which made up the form, and the whole form beautifully expresses the containment and the pouring out of liquid (Figure 64).

The body of the pitcher relates to the jar and the bottle. It is usually bulbous, full, and rounded, giving the feeling of capacity. Its interior space is generous. As in the jar, the hollow of the pitcher seems to exert pressure outward. Even rather narrow pitchers may have this quality of space enclosed. The profile of the body may have a rising movement toward a shoulder, or it may be spherical, lozenge-shaped or have a low center of gravity like a gourd standing upright. The body is to hold, to keep.

The constriction of the neck guards the liquid in the body. It prevents splashing and spilling. It preserves the cool and dark of the interior, limiting access to insects or dirt. The neck may take the form of an inward sweep of the profile, or it may be more like a collar. In pitchers intended for water the neck is usually quite wide, those meant for oils, essences, or liquors are usually narrower.

The handle and the spout grow out of the neck, balancing and complementing each other. The spout breaks the rim of the neck, giving a path and direction to the outward flow of liquid. It surmounts the constriction of the neck with a channel for release. Opposite the spout the handle sprouts from the neck, springing outward and down to rejoin the body, making a space for the hand just above where the neck emerges from the body.

FORMING A PITCHER

Making a pitcher on the wheel starts out with procedures similar to those used for making jars or bottles. A cylinder is formed, no wider than required to admit the hand. The bottom is carefully formed, and if no trimming is planned, as much clay as possible is moved up into the piece or cut away with the stick. When the cylinder has been raised and brought to the right thickness throughout, the lower part is bellied out. At first this is done by pulls in which the inside hand dominates and presses outward. The proportion of body to neck is thus established. The diameter of the neck is disturbed or enlarged as little as possible during the forming of the lower part. Final shaping of the body may be done with the profile tool, which can be es-

81

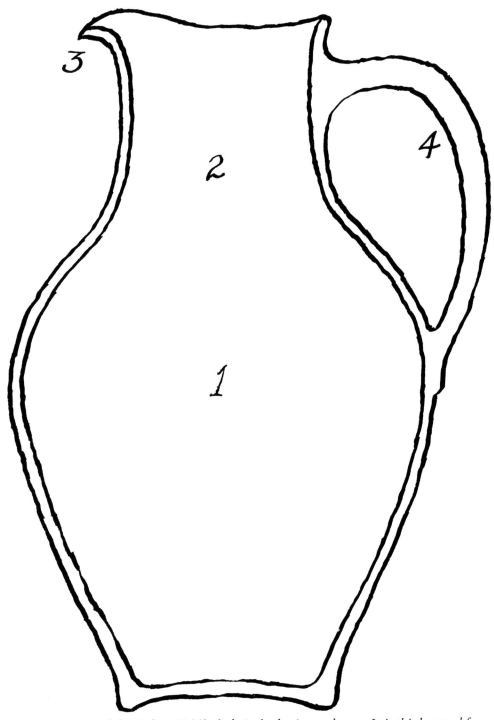

Fig. 64   Parts of the pitcher: (1) The body is the dominant element. It is thinly potted for correct weight; (2) Neck forms a constriction narrow enough to prevent splash yet open enough to permit cleaning; (3) Spout grows out of rim. Its edge is stretched downward to prevent dripping; (4) Handle bridges area between neck and body and offers ample hand space.

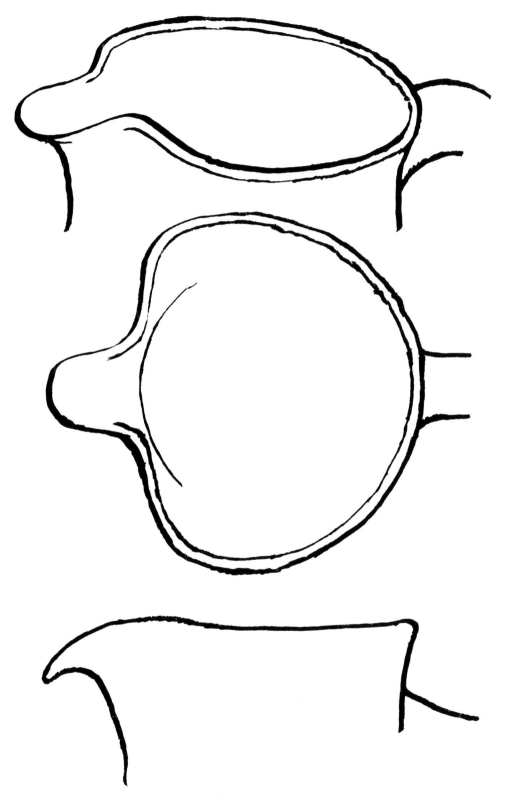

Fig. 65   Pouring spout.

83

pecially useful in pressing out the shoulder or upper part of the body.

Attention is now given to the neck. It may have become off center or overly wide during the forming of the body. Truing up, thinning, collaring in, and shaping bring the neck form to completion. The character of the pitcher will depend to a great extent on the relationship between body and neck and especially on the transition between them. If the clay becomes very wet or if the throwing process is too prolonged, the curve or turn from body to neck can become weak, loose, and lacking in structure (Figure 66).

The lip can be given a pronounced outward turn, and this makes it easier to form the spout. To form the spout, a section of the lip is steadied with the thumb and first finger of the left hand while the first finger of the right hand pulls and stretches the clay downward into a groove or channel. Several gentle strokes are needed to make a deep, well-formed spout (Figure 67). For effective pouring, the lip of the spout is sharpened and drawn downward until the surface just below the lip is "uphill" for the pouring liquid (Figure 65). This will prevent the last few drops from running over the lip and down the side of the pitcher. The spout is made wide enough to channel and direct a reasonable volume of pour. If it is too wide, however, the pitcher will be hard to "aim." Below the spout there may be a throat. It is a slight distortion of the neck made by pressure from one finger inside running from the spout to the body below. This throat or gentle groove beneath the spout serves to open the neck and to prevent a visual effect sometimes seen in pitchers, a choked or constricted feeling that results from a slightly collapsed area near the spout. A loose mouthed, or gaping effect may occur at the spout. This results in the spout being pulled out away from the neck in a way that distorts the upper part of the neck into an oval. The potter must feel his way between the extremes of loose, soft looking spouts and tight, neat, controlled ones.

FINISHING A PITCHER

Exclusive of the handle, the pitcher may be finished completely on the wheel and cut off with the wire. (Actually, small pitchers which can be grasped around the neck function perfectly well without handles.) It is really satisfying to make them this way, but more often than not the pitcher will be somewhat thick toward the bottom and will benefit from some trimming. The stiffened pot is recentered right side up on the wheel head and with a syringe a bit of water is run under it. This sticks the piece down temporarily. The lower part of the piece is then shaved down, with perhaps a bead or accent left at the foot. Cut foot rings seem unnecessary in pitchers, but if one is to be made, the pitcher is centered upside down for trimming. Here the spout will create difficulties because it interrupts the level of the lip. This can be overcome by padding under the pitcher with wads of clay on the wheel head. If the piece is not trimmed, a pleasing and functional bottom edge can be made by rolling as shown in Figure 68.

The pitcher with its wide bottom surmounted with a narrower neck gives a logical place for the handle to begin and to end, and provides an inviting space for the hand. The scale, shape, and placement of the handle are important to both the functioning and the appearance of the piece. The handle can originate from the neck just below the rim, or it can grow out of the rim. Making it come from the rim usually requires some hand modelling to complete the attachment and, for this reason, in shops where speed is a factor the handles are placed a little below the rim. The form of the pitcher itself usually suggests the right place for the handle's lower attachment. There are choices. Will the handle rise upwards from its attachment or move directly outward? Will the handle be wide and straplike, or more narrow and rounded? Will it make a wide vigorous sweep or keep close in to the form? Will it be a continuous curve or a curve which is drawn into a straight line in its lower half? Ways of making handles are discussed in the following section.

The balance of the pitcher involves factors so subtle as to defy description. Proportion and weight have much to do with it, as does the scale and placement of the handle. If the pitcher is very high in relation to its width, balance may be awkward with too much effort required for tipping and pouring. On the other hand, a wide horizontal piece may be hard to hold steadily in the hand. Pitchers and teapots can have a quality which I call "eagerness to pour." An exaggerated forward movement of the spout may express the pouring function vividly, perhaps to the point of an appearance of restlessness which contradicts the primary function of containment.

The pitcher form, consisting of the basic elements of body, neck, spout, and handle, can be expressed in many different proportions and styles (Figure 70). In the classic form, as described above, the neck grows out of the body through a curving transition (Figures 75 and 77). Another type, less common, has a more distinct articulation or separation between the neck and the body (Figure 78). The effect of this is something akin to the articulation found so frequently in the plant world where one form grows from another, but with a distinct zone of change. The neck of the pitcher may be a distinctly separate form, a drum shape or cylinder arising out of the globular body. Such a distinctly articulated neck is a very obvious place for the upper handle attachment, and the spout can be made on its rim without disturbing the rotund quality of the main form. If this neck is made short it can look somewhat like a collar, and the spout can be made to relate to it like a necktie. On a neck like this, the spout can have a precise and bounded form. Pitchers with fat bodies and short necks are commodious.

Some pitchers are nearly cylindrical. The sides are more or less straight

Fig. 66 *Pitcher form. Even before the spout and handle are added, the form expresses volume and containment in the body, constriction in the neck, and pouring or giving out in the outward-turned lip. In this stage, the lip may seem to curve outward excessively, but the spout modifies this.*
Fig. 67 *Pulling the spout.*

Fig. 68   Rolling the pitcher
to finish the bottom edge.
Fig. 69   Pulling the handle
on the pitcher.

and the traditional articulation between body and neck hardly exists (Figure 76). Such a pitcher is easily cleaned and has a simple, direct character. It can be given a more elegant appearance by making it tall and narrow, but this elongation, if carried too far, upsets the balance and limits capacity.

The pitcher is one of those hand pieces we become acquainted with not only by vision but also through tactile encounter and a sensing of weight and balance. The pitcher is an extension of the hand. Pouring is giving out, passing along. The form of the pitcher originated in its usefulness as a vessel in pouring milk, water, oil, and beer. It has been a fixture of the kitchen and the tavern, a homey, sometimes homely pot, definitely more modest in its pretensions to art or beauty than the vase. We like our favorite pitcher in somewhat the same way we like an old pipe or a worn pair of shoes. Pitchers were much in use at the well heads of medieval English towns, for many of them dropped accidentally into the wells and have later been recovered intact during excavations for buildings and roads. The pitcher as an adjunct to washing and bathing survived until fairly recently in the pitcher and bowl wash stand set. Modern packaging and refrigeration are lessening the need for pitchers, but they remain a favorite of potters.

Pots which are not pitchers can, of course, be used for pouring. The ancient Greek *lekythos* and the *amphora* were obviously used for pouring even though they did not have spouts. The ancestor of all pitchers is perhaps the Greek *oinochoe,* which was made at least as early as the seventh century B.C. It has a well-developed spout, with handle opposite.

The term jug usually means a vessel for liquids with a handle and a small neck but without a spout for pouring. However, the terms pitcher and jug are sometimes used interchangeably.

The pitcher, common and popular in Europe, was relatively rare in the Orient. The Japanese seldom made pieces with handles of any sort, and apparently never made pitchers until Western models were copied. The unimportance of milk as a food in China and Japan may account for this.

Fig. 70   Pitcher forms.

15 HANDLES

Only a few pottery forms require handles. These are the drinking and pouring vessels, the pitcher, teapot, cup, mug, and jug. However, the handle has assumed an importance to pottery design which goes much beyond mere function. It has been used to accent, to give scale, to enliven, and to add linear elements to the normally rather compact and centered form of pots.

The pottery handle begins as a ropelike or straplike piece of clay and can be made in a number of ways. Perhaps the easiest way is simply to roll out a coil of clay. The ancient Greeks made many of their handles this way. The thickness of the coil can easily be varied so as to make one or both ends of the handle thicker than the middle section. The coils can also be braided, twisted together, or fastened together side by side to make handles of complex structure. Straplike handles can be cut out of a flat slab of clay and given various textures by rubbing or modelling.

The seldom used handle cutter is a stout oval loop of metal fastened to a wooden holder. This loop is dragged through a lump of clay to cut a long snake which is then cut to the right length and applied to the pot. A stout wire modelling tool can be adapted by bending to serve as a handle cutter. The trouble with a handle cut this way is that it is uniform in cross section, having no taper or variation in its form.

Handles can be made by cutting strips from thrown cylinders. The throwing can be planned to take advantage of the finger marks, thus providing ridges or striations. But making cylinders just to cut up for handles involves some wasted effort.

Pulling handles from a lump of clay is easy, quick, and results in a functional and pleasing form. A ball of soft clay about the size and shape of a pear is held in the left hand. With plenty of water for lubrication, the clay is pulled downward with the right hand in a series of movements which both squeeze and extend the clay (Figure 71). At first the developing handle can be made round in cross section, but as it thins it can be flattened into more of a strap by pulling the clay between the thumb and the lower part of the first finger. If the pulling is done gradually with many strokes, a natural taper will

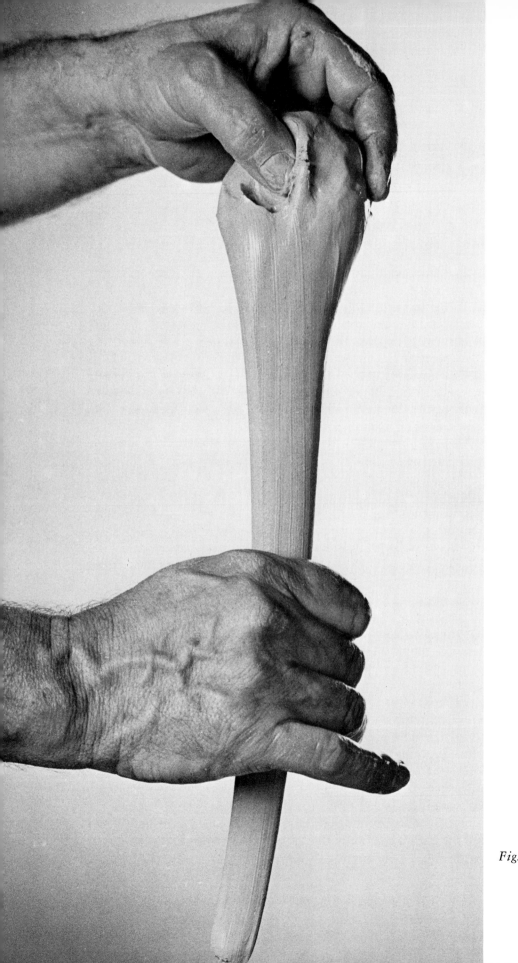

Fig. 71 Pulling a ha

develop. When the handle has been extended to the desired length and section, it is allowed to curve into a loop and is set up to stiffen, still part of the ball of clay from which it was pulled (Figures 72 and 73).

The curve which a pulled handle naturally assumes is usually very similar to the curve it will have on the finished pot. The clay seems to want to loop over in just the right form. The pulled handle, when well done, has a fluid, dynamic quality. It can be soft and claylike without being mushy or irregular.

When the handle has stiffened somewhat, it is cut off from its stump with the knife. The cut can be accurately made for the upper attachment, using just the right angle. Excess length is left at the end.

Putting a handle on a pot requires considerable dexterity. If the operation is uncertain or prolonged, a certain muddiness and confusion results. Direct and confident craftsmanship produces attachments which are simple, fresh, and claylike. The upper attachment is made first; the handle is squeezed onto the pot after the joint end has been buttered with slip. The handle seems to drop down and find for itself the best place for the lower attachment. The excess length can be pinched or cut off.

Instead of making a finished handle first and fastening it to the pot as described above, the handle can be pulled on the piece (Figure 69). A blank, or short stub of a handle is first made by pulling. This is made thicker and shorter than the intended final form. Or the blank can be made by rolling a ball of clay until it assumes the form of short tapered coil, perhaps half as long as the handle will be. The handle-to-be is set aside to dry and stiffen a bit. It is then firmly pressed against the pot to make the upper attachment. Since the stump is still soft and plastic, little or no slip is required. The attachment is strengthened by squeezing the clay forward against the wall of the pot, making the form of the handle merge with that of the pot. Next, pulling is begun. This is made easier if the piece is held in such a way as to make the handle droop straight down. Pulling must be done carefully and rather gingerly to avoid pulling the handle off the pot or developing thin places. Plenty of time must be allowed; if the process is too hurried or abrupt the even taper from attachment to end will be lost. When the handle has been given the desired shape and length, it is curved around and the bottom attachment made. Some excess length makes it easier to get the right loop and to make a strong lower joint. The good thing about a handle which is pulled on the pot, rather than being made separately and then attached, is the integrated relationship which is developed between handle and pot. The upper attachment can be made so the handle seems to grow out of the pot in a natural way and the joint can suggest strength and firmness (Figure 74).

Some forms, like the traditional pitcher, with its transition from the bulging lower part to the smaller neck, present a very obvious position for a handle. On other pieces the placement may be more problematical. Handles

91

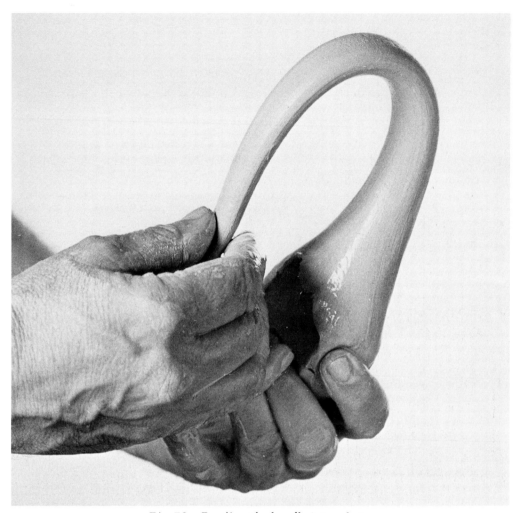

Fig. 72 Bending the handle into a loop.

Fig. 73   *The handle set up to stiffen.*

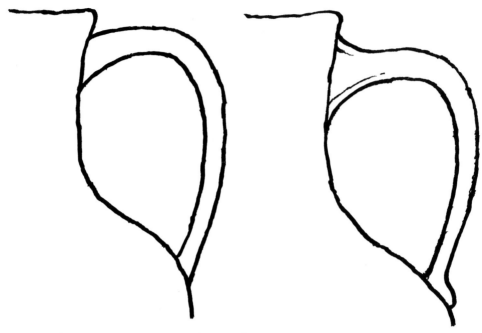

Fig. 74   Handle attachments.

seem to be more at home toward the upper part of a form than lower down. Small handles give an enhanced sense of scale to a piece. Large handles and ones which loop far out from the form tend to make the form hyperactive or even aggressive.

The handle may grow vigorously away from the body of the pot and trace a curve full of energy and movement, but it returns, closing the circle, completing the circuit.

The curve of a handle can be lively, dynamic, and forceful, as for example, the handles on many ancient Greek pots. Some of these handles rise dramatically upwards from the lip of the piece and then curve over and down in a graceful loop. Or the curve of the handle can be quiet and slow, turning downward and staying close in to the form of the pot. This feeling of closeness and simplicity in the handle has been favored by potters making wares for hard everyday use where the handle is always the first thing to break. The form of a handle is usually in marked contrast to the form of the pot itself. Whereas the pot is hollow, swelling, compact, and voluminous, the handle is springlike, linear, moving, and liquid. Handles and pots are complementary parts of a whole. If the handle grows too far away from the pot it becomes a thing in itself—and the unity of the piece is lost. Pottery handles have been likened to the limbs of trees, which grow out of the trunk as a distinct and separate branch yet preserve a structural and organic connection. Of course the limb, unlike a handle, grows with and from the tree and is not something which has been attached. One might also think of the arm, which arises out of the shoulder and articulates into a form which is distinct from the torso but which could not conceivably have an existence apart from the rest of the body (Figure 79).

The taper of a handle from the upper part to the lower answers the need for more strength at the top where the weight of the pot is actually held. It seems right that the upper attachment should be relatively thick, and the lower attachment more delicate and thin, and this comes about naturally with the pulled handle. Handles which have a somewhat straplike form work better than ones which are rounded in cross section. The latter are slippery in the grasp.

All the details of the handle, the attachments, the treatment of the "tail" or leftover length at the bottom, the striations or ridges, the marks of finger or tool, are toned down and minimized by firing shrinkage and a coating of glaze. For this reason, the features of the handle are stated more boldly in the fresh pot than they are to appear in the finished piece.

Handles might be considered a necessary evil, mere functional additions which distract from the main body of the pot. Actually, handles can enhance, enliven, complete, and punctuate the form. Handles have been made in an endless variety of ways, sometimes in imitation of twigs or tangled vines, twisted rope, or sculptured animals or reptiles. Handles have been an expression of exuberance and whimsy and often appear on urns, tureens, and vases where they are not really needed.

Handles occur much more frequently on European pottery than on pottery made in China, Korea, and Japan. Cups and pitchers with handles were a rarity in the Orient. This is perhaps the result of a preference in the Orient for picking up pottery directly in the hands.

The pulled handle seems to be a European invention and is never seen on Chinese, Japanese, Greek, or Persian pottery. It is possible that the technique of handle-pulling originated with the German potters of the Rhine region; in any case, as early as the sixteenth century they were making salt-glazed jugs and mugs with beautifully made pulled handles. It is hard to find a parallel in any other craft to the pulled handle. It is a form made not only by hand but in the hand, and the actual gesture used in producing the form is almost identical to the gesture involved in its use.

Fig. 75 Pitcher. The body was quickly thrown; prominent throwing marks remain. Evidence of some trimming can be seen at the bottom. Body and neck are not greatly different in diameter, and the form rises from bottom to top in uninterrupted curves. The handle is close to the neck.

Fig. 76 Pitcher. The bottom is broad and flat, giving maximum stability. The neck takes the form of a constriction under the lip, rather than an articulated, cylindrical passage.

Fig. 77 Pitcher. This piece is
similar to the pitcher in Figure 75. Here, the body swells
out prominently, dominating
the neck. Although the body
and the neck flow into each
other, there is a pronounced
shoulder.

Fig. 78 Pitcher. The body
and the neck are potted as distinctly articulated but related
forms, with an accented break
between them. The body swells
and pushes outward, while
the neck has a concave profile.
The spout is a feature be-
longing with the neck.

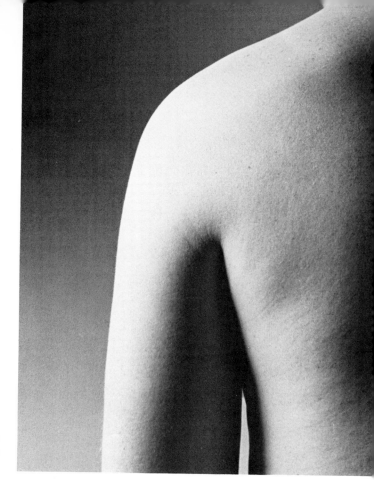

Fig. 79 Shoulder. A lesson in the organic relationship of parts to whole.

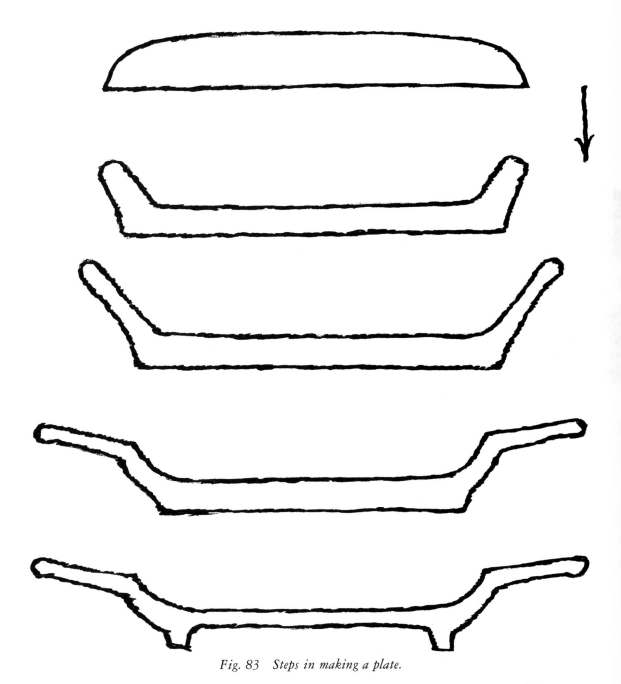

Fig. 83   Steps in making a plate.

once irregularities have developed. As the plate takes form, enough clay must be carried out to the rim to provide proper thickness and strength there, avoiding a paper-thin edge.

As in the case of low bowls, when a plate dries, the rim curls upward making the form higher than it was when first made. Therefore the rim must be made lower to compensate for this change. There is some guesswork in this because if the rim is made too low, it may not rise at all during drying or may even turn downward making an impossibly flat plate.

HAND-FORMING ON THE WHEEL

Making plates by hand on the wheel is actually quite difficult. Not only are there difficulties in forming; drying and firing also cause trouble. The first step toward successful drying is to release the plate from the bat or surface upon which it was made as soon as possible. The wire is passed under the plate right after it is finished. It is best to make plates on plywood or composition board bats which can be removed from the wheel. Then the plate can stiffen before any attempt is made to pick it up or turn it over. The plate

must be dried slowly in a draft-free atmosphere. If one side dries more rapidly than the other, warping will result. As soon as the plate is stiff enough to handle without distortion, it is turned over.

TRIMMING

Trimming should begin as soon as the bottom is stiff enough to resist slumping under the pressure of the trimming tool. As in the case of bowls, the bottom surface is cut to conform to the inside; the foot is carved out as a projecting ring. The broad expanse of the plate, the wide foot, and the subtle rise of the form at the rim make the plate much the most difficult pottery form to trim, and many of the ineptitudes seen in plate design are caused by failures in trimming.

Plates may be too thick, too thin, or have a foot ring that is either too large or too small in diameter. One very common difficulty is a droop in the bottom. This results in what is known to potters as a "spinner," a plate which rests on some point in the bottom other than the foot. This can be prevented by cutting a higher foot and giving a slight upwards bend to the surface inside the foot. This upwards bend or dome in the middle of the plate tends to subside in the firing, slumping down just sufficiently, it is hoped, to give a flat surface.

STRENGTHENING FEATURES

To survive the fire and to function properly, the plate must have a certain architectural stability. Some of the features of the cross section of a plate are shown in Figure 85: (1) thickening or bead at the rim helps prevent warping and gives the finished plate more strength and resistance to chipping; it also makes the plate easier to pick up; (2) the rim is sufficiently high to make the plate easy to pick up; additional height is provided to compensate for any slumping during firing; (3) the form thickens near the foot, which gives added strength and resistance to slumping in the fire; (4) the foot is placed at the point where the rise of the plate begins; it is high enough to keep the bottom off the table; (5) the bottom is made slightly thinner than the rise outside the foot and is slightly domed upward.

FIRING PROBLEMS

A variety of difficulties are brought on by firing. Plates slump, warp, stick to the kiln shelves, crack open in the middle or on the rim. Control of these problems depends on the firing procedures and the kind of clay used, especially the degree of vitrification. Careful drying can prevent some losses. Cracks developing in the center of the plate, a common disease, are usually

Fig. 84 Opposite. *Throwing a plate.*

caused by letting the rim dry faster than the surface inside the foot. For example, if a plate is made on a wet plaster bat and left on it until the rim begins to dry, center cracks will develop because the center part will dry last. Since it is held prisoner in the already stiffened perimeter it can only accommodate shrinkage by cracking. Getting the plate off the bat as soon as possible and drying it evenly helps to prevent bottom cracks. But if they persist, it may be necessary to add some stiffer clay to the bottom area during throwing. This is done by wedging up some clay stiffer than that being used for throwing and making from it a flattened piece about the size and shape of a thick cookie. After the clay has been opened up and the bottom formed, the cookie of stiffer clay is placed in the center and pounded down flat with a wooden tool.

Another remedy for center cracks is to bury a circular piece of cheesecloth or open weave fiber glass cloth in the clay.

PLATE TYPES

There are several kinds of plates (Figure 86). The high coup plate is near the borderline between the plate and the bowl. Its inside surface curves from the very center, rising slowly but continuously to the rim. The foot is relatively narrow. The form is graceful and curvaceous. This type of plate is favored in China and Japan. These flat plates were seldom used for food because chopsticks are awkward to use on a flat surface; there is no place to gather up the food. The coup plate was used more for passing and for serving than to eat from. Since no cutting was done on the plate, its foot could be quite small and still give sufficient stability. A high foot made the plate easy to pick up.

The low coup plate has a flat central surface. It then rises in a smooth curve to the edge. It is simple, easy to clean, and has a large capacity for its diameter. Its simple form, without breaks or ridges to catch the light, makes it an unobtrusive, almost featureless object. The low coup plate stacks efficiently, one plate nestling down into the other.

The rim plate has a well or bowl at the center and from this a flat rim extends outward, usually canted up somewhat. The rim may have originated as a place to keep condiments, sweets and the like away from the rest of the food. It also makes the plate easy to pick up without getting the thumbs in the food. The rim offers a flat and distinctly bounded area for a band of decoration surrounding the central surface. If the center of the plate is decorated, the rim functions as a frame. Compared to the coup plate, the rim plate has, for its diameter, less real capacity and less space for cutting food. Cutting food at the table seems to be a European custom, and the plate as it has evolved provides a broad flat area and a wide foot which keeps the plate from tipping.

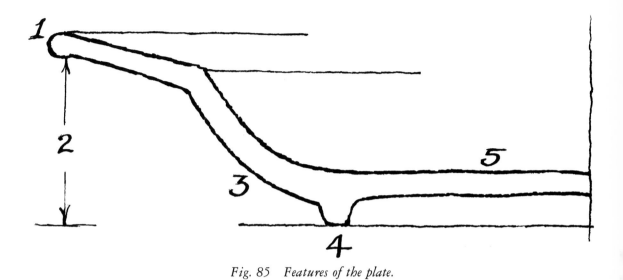

Fig. 85   Features of the plate.

Fig. 86   Plate forms in cross section.

Pottery Form

Persian and Hispano-Mooresque plates sometimes have a mound or lump in the middle as big as half a tennis ball. The custom was for several persons to share one plate of food, and the high place in the middle solves the problem of who gets the last bite. It is sure not to remain in the exact center but to roll toward one of the diners.

Plates should stack well, and this requires careful design to enable one plate to nestle into the next. For good stacking, hand-made plates are usually inferior to those made on the jigger or from molds, because no matter how carefully the plates are made on the wheel some irregularities will result from firing. This, added to the distortions of drying and firing, will inevitably produce crooked stacking rather than a neat sequence of uniformly spaced rims. This may not be important but it can increase sales resistance. Many studio potters avoid making plates because of the difficulties in forming and firing and the resulting high losses. The potter can seldom profit from plate-making unless the plates are made as individual pieces designed as vehicles for decoration.

DECORATION

As a surface for decoration, the plate has served as the potter's canvas or drawing paper. The challenge of adapting designs to a circular area has been met in countless ways. Unlike the artist's picture, which must be hung on a wall and properly lighted to be really seen, the plate as an object creates its own small environment. The circular plate is a focusing disc trained on the beholder. Not meant to be seen from any specific angle and often covered with food or fruit, the design on a plate makes a modest demand on our attention. Its pictorial dimension is secondary to its obvious function as a container. For this reason, unpretentious graphic or pictorial expressions seem at home on plates. The very limitation imposed on the decorator by the plate has often yielded benefits in charm, spontaneity, humor, and delicacy. A vast number of pictorial impulses from naive folk art to work by Picasso have been realized on plates.

17 LARGE POTS

Most pots are what might be called medium-sized objects. Pieces which are less than about 2 inches high (plates and flat forms excepted) are miniatures. At the other end of the scale, pots which are more than 24 inches high could be called large. From a purely functional standpoint, and as pottery is used in present-day culture, very large pots have a limited usefulness. They are hard to move about, subject to breaking, and they occupy space needed for other things. Vessels of metal, plastic, concrete, or wood are generally more practical for water, storage, or planting.

In ancient times, large pottery jars and containers were used because there was no practical alternative. Metals were scarce and had to be worked by hand-forging. Plastics were unknown. The wooden barrel with staves and hoops had not been invented and in any case would have been too expensive for most uses. Pottery was used for grain storage; for wine-making, storage, and transport; for pickling; and for water. The Greeks used vast numbers of large pottery amphoras for their extensive overseas wine trade. These tall narrow bottles have no foot or flat place at the bottom and thus cannot stand by themselves. Presumably they were packed on shipboard lying down like wood in a cord, probably with cushions of straw in between. The production of these wine bottles was the bread-and-butter of the Greek pottery industry. We can be sure that plenty of them did break in service, and the ones which sank with ships are still being brought up by divers. At the palace of Knossos in Crete there still exist a battery of enormous pottery storage jars which were used for grain storage. These jars, six feet and more in height, probably functioned well in keeping grain free of rot and vermin. Similar granaries of large pottery vessels must have been common in the ancient world. Another use for large pots was olive curing and olive oil storage. On Crete, large pots are still made for olive pickling. They are more resistant to the corrosive effects of the salt brine than either metal or wood. Pickling jars are still widely used in Korea. Large, handsome pots hold the *kimchi,* or pickled vegetables, which are a staple part of the Korean diet. Almost every Korean household has a collection of them in various sizes.

FORMING LARGE PIECES
Making and firing very large pots is a challenge. All of the difficulties of

the craft are compounded by large scale. Molds are not an easy solution to making large forms because the mold itself must be even larger, and therefore hard to make, as well as heavy and difficult to fill and empty in slip-casting.

Coiling and modelling, although slow, are the easiest methods for making large forms. No particular difficulties will be met in hand building on a large scale by the method of adding coils or wads. The form is built gradually, developing upwards as it grows. In order to have enough strength in the lower part to support the upper part, the clay must be allowed to stiffen as the work proceeds. The unequal degree of dryness between the lower section and the newly added clay can result in stresses severe enough to cause cracking. The relative dryness or wetness of all sections of a large piece must be carefully controlled. An atomizer is used to dampen parts which are getting too dry, and coverings of wet cloths or plastics are applied to areas which are to be kept damp. Large pieces must be dried very slowly in a draft-free situation. Hand building is discussed in detail in section 23.

THROWING LARGE PIECES

Increased scale makes throwing enormously more difficult. For this reason, perhaps, the ability to make a very large thrown pot has been taken by some as a measure of a potter's skill. Everyone reaches his limit of scale at some point, and even potters of legendary prowess come up against the inherent limitation of the clay. When it reaches a certain height, a thrown cylinder of a given clay must collapse because the soft walls at the bottom can no longer support the weight above. Gravity works against the potter. Sheldon Carey, contemporary American potter, developed a clever device for getting around this condition. It is a wheel which can be turned upside down. After the clay is centered and a thick cylinder made, the position of the wheel is reversed. From then on the pot is developing downward instead of up, and gravity assists rather than inhibits the extension of the cylinder.

Several stratagems may be employed for achieving large thrown pieces. The clay must be highly plastic and contain enough granular particles to furnish "tooth." Smooth clay, no matter how plastic, will not stand in tall cylinders. The wheel should be low, giving the potter a position above his work. Centering is made easier if the clay is patted on center first. This is done by running the wheel at a slow speed and spanking the clay lightly with both palms as it revolves. The ball may also be hollowed out by striking the center lightly with the fist many times as the ball turns. The final centering and hollowing is done with the wheel going fast. When the cylinder is being raised, as little water as possible is used. Some potters use a sponge in both the right and the left hand to minimize the need for lubricant. The walls of the cylinder must be kept straight because on a tall piece the slightest bulge will develop into a slump. Care is taken to prevent thin places developing in the cylinder, especially in the lower part. The lower part is kept quite thick to furnish support for the clay above, and some trimming of this extra clay is usually necessary later. All shaping must be delayed until the cylinder is raised and thinned.

Bigger is not necessarily better. The large pot frequently fails because of the struggle which has gone into its making, a struggle in which the subtleties of form are apt to suffer. Pots of modest scale, even though not exciting in form, may have the virtue of usefulness. But the large pot, if it has little or no real function, must stand as an object which justifies itself, an object for contemplation only. And those qualities which make a pot a thing of value aside from function are the very ones which are likely to get lost in the process of throwing on a large scale.

COIL AND THROW METHOD

If speed is not essential, it may be better to make large pieces by additive processes rather than by throwing from a single lump of clay. The form and cross section can then be made to emerge more in response to the potter's sensitive impulses and less as a result of the struggle with gravity and with the recalcitrant nature of the clay. A method commonly used in Japan for making large pieces is the coil and throw method. The lower part of the pot is thrown as usual from one piece of clay. It reaches up to perhaps one-fourth or one-third of the eventual finished height. This lower section is set aside to stiffen. It is not allowed to reach the leather hard state, however, and is still flexible when work on it begins again. Next, a heavy coil or rope of soft clay is laid on the top edge and joined well by pinching and smearing. The joint of the coil is carefully welded together and smoothed. Throwing is begun again, and the new section made from the coil may raise the height by six inches or more. In this process, the upper edge may become rather ragged and uneven, but this can be leveled with a needle cut.

Proceeding in this manner, one coil at a time with some drying of each new section, a pot of any size can be made. The shape is under complete control. The shaping, however, must be done progressively in stages from the bottom to the top, and there is no opportunity at the end of the process to correct or develop the form as a whole. In this sense, the coil and throw method depends more on what might be called design, or the visualization of the form beforehand, than does throwing. The method also takes a lot of patience. Time must be allowed for each stage to stiffen. The shape appears gradually rather than suddenly.

VARIATIONS ON COIL AND THROW

In the Korean variation of the coil and throw method, long slabs or ribbons of clay are added instead of round coils. More clay is added each time and thus more growth is achieved. A narrow slab, perhaps three times as thick as the eventual wall of the pot, is rolled out on the floor or table. It is

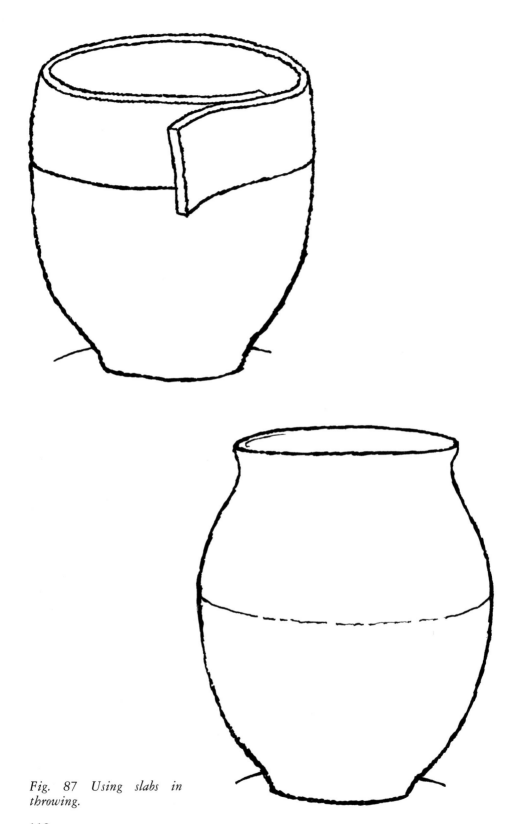

Fig. 87 Using slabs in throwing.

112

made somewhat longer than the circumference of the piece to which it is to be added. It can be made uniform in thickness by rolling between two guide sticks with the rolling pin. The slab, perhaps six or eight inches wide, is then rolled up for ease of handling and unrolled as it is laid and fastened to the upper rim of the unfinished pot. The ends are made to overlap, then are cut, both ends together, with the needle. This gives a neat joint without lumps. This way of making a slab addition makes further shaping and throwing quite easy because the slab is already flat and uniform in thickness and is therefore not so apt to become irregular (Figures 87 and 88). In the Korean *kimchi* jar shop, pots four feet tall are made by this method and with amazing speed. An assistant makes the slabs on the floor and hands them to the thrower at the right moment. An oil lamp is hung down inside the developing pot to hasten drying and stiffening as the work proceeds. After it is in place, each added slab or ribbon is lightly beaten and then thrown, usually with a gain in height of about twelve inches. By the time the last section is added and the pot is finished at the top, the bottom section is quite stiff. The whole piece is then lifted off the wheel and rolled along the floor like a barrel to the drying area.

THROWING AND COILING COMBINED

Japanese potters sometimes make cylinders by the coil and throw method and then while the cylinder is still soft throw the form in the usual way. The bottom of the cylinder is made by beating out a cookie of clay on the wheel head. Then coils are added, each coil being carefully pinched on and then thrown, until a straight-sided cylinder of the desired height is made. Since the cylinder is made up of smoothed coils, it naturally has some irregularities, but these get ironed out later. The potter then wets the cylinder, which is still soft, and throws the form exactly as if he had made the cylinder from one lump. The advantage of this method is that the cylinder, since it is not made by throwing, can be relatively stiff, and the shaping can be done without the usual danger of collapse from softness due to overwetting. The disadvantage is the slowness of the method and the likelihood that irregularities from the coils will persist in the finished piece.

TWO-STAGE CYLINDERS

In some European pottery shops, large pieces are thrown from a cylinder which is made in two stages (Figure 90). First, a cylinder without a bottom is made on the wheel. To make it easier to pick up, a temporary top is made of a light slab of clay, stuck onto the lip. Immediately after throwing and with the temporary top on, the cylinder is cut off with the wire and is lifted to a waiting bat which has been lightly dusted with dry clay to prevent sticking. Then a second cylinder of the same diameter is made. This will be the lower part of the pot and it has a bottom. The lip of this second cylinder is buttered with slip and the first cylinder is picked up and added to the second, care being taken to line up the two forms exactly (Figure 92). This method results

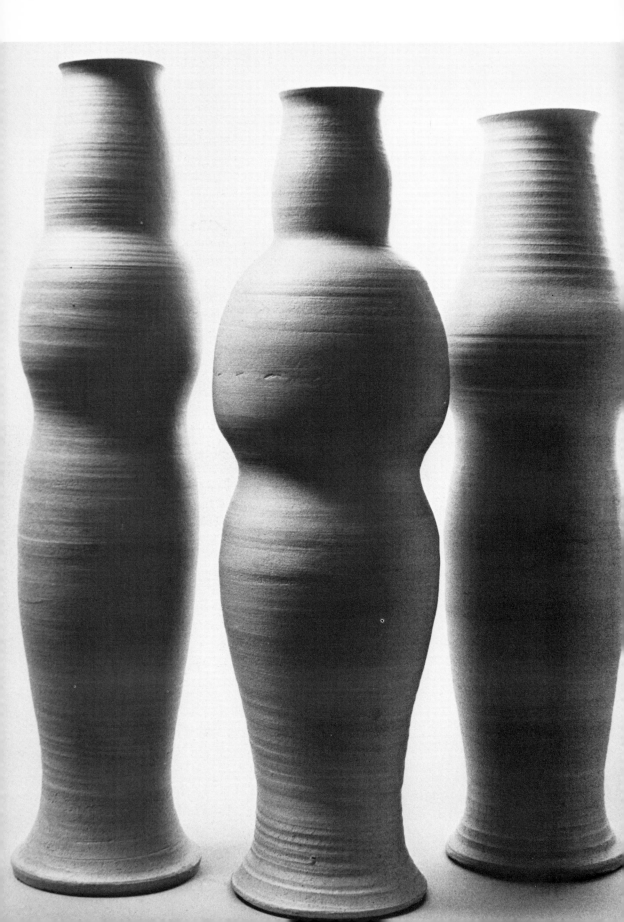

18 POTS WITH LIDS

A lid on a pot furnishes cover and closure of the form. It makes an open-mouthed jar into a more compact, sealed vessel, one which holds its hollow in dark reserve. Whereas the jar breathes in the air from above and invites ingress and egress, the covered pot encloses its own bit of space. The open pot may seem a bit incomplete when not in use; its shape suggests content. But the covered pot with its secret interior is a completed thing. It is rounded out sculpturally, a dimensional form positive in all of its aspects.

Some covered pots are made so the lid and the pot are part of a continuous form. The profile of the pot may be continued in the lid, with a flowing transition (Figure 98). In other covered pots, the lid serves less as a completion of the form and more as an accent. The lid may be a counterpoint to the pot—a punctuation and a surprise.

The knob of the lid can be modest, functional, and intended to keep its place as a subordinate part of the design. Or it may be a strong or even dominant note. Lids can grow on pots in many ways. It is like the integral parts of a plant: stem, blossom, or fruit.

In Figure 93, some of the various kinds of pottery lids are shown: (1), (2), and (3) are recessed lids. These can be thrown right side up from the hump and cut off so that very little if any trimming is required (Figures 95 and 96). They need no flange because the lid is shaped to settle down in the opening of the pot, where it finds a secure seat. The knob is made from a little ball which is reserved in the center right at the start of throwing. It can be made hollow as shown in (2). Actually the knob can be eliminated if the rim of the lid is small enough in diameter to be picked up easily and if the rim extends a bit beyond the edge of the pot for firm grip. In (3), a socket or seat has been made on the pot which receives the lid. This, combined with the recess which drops slightly into the hole, results in a lid which does not fall off easily, a good feature for teapots (Figure 100). In (4), there is a flange on the lid which fits down into the opening of the pot. This type of lid is thrown upside down and the flange is measured to fit the opening.

The lid must be finished by trimming, and the knob is either carved out of the excess clay or made separately and attached. Lids of this kind are usually made where a high dome is desired. The process of throwing it is much like making a low bowl or plate. It is easier to form the flange if it begins to take shape early in throwing. The clay is drawn out to the right diameter as meas-

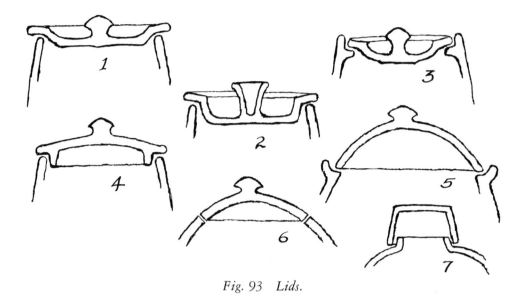

Fig. 93 Lids.

ured with the callipers. As in the case of bowls, the lid is made somewhat flatter than the desired final shape to allow for the shrinkage upwards and inward. After both pot and lid have stiffened, the lid can be cut off its bat and put in place on the pot. It can then be trimmed in place, which is an aid to getting it the right shape. The thickness can be checked from time to time just by lifting up the lid, then putting it back in its seat for further trimming.

The flange may be part of the pot rather than part of the lid as shown in (5). To make this flange requires a little advanced planning in the early stages of throwing. A thickening at the lip must be maintained when the pot is being pulled up. At the end of shaping, the thickened upper edge is divided into lip and flange. A flat seat for the lid can be refined by holding a wooden tool against the surface of the lip as the pot revolves. A pot with a flange may be provided with a lid made either right side up or upside down as in (1) and (4). But a flange need not be made on the lid. The lid in this case can be, in effect, a shallow bowl with a knob instead of a foot. If the flange is on the pot, the lid can settle down into a recess in a way that indicates that the pot and lid were really made for each other.

In (6), the lid is made by cutting out the top of an enclosed form much as one would cut the lid of a jack-o-lantern. The pot is made by drawing in the top until it is closed and forms a knob of the desired size and shape. After the piece has stiffened a bit, the lid is cut with the needle. A slanting cut favors a better seat, but no matter how you cut it, the seat on this kind of lid is uncertain. Three small tabs of clay can be added to the lower edge of the lid to improve its grip on the pot.

Cap lids as shown in (7), Figure 93, were originally made by the Chinese for tea jars (Figure 99). The cap served also as a measure for the tea. A collar is provided on the pot over which the cap fits. The cap is made upside down as if it were a small straight-sided pot.

Getting lids to fit well is a test of the potter's skill and control. Measurements are made when the pot is freshly thrown. Drawing the shape of the lid out to just the right size requires judgment as to just how much clay to use and a knowledge of how the lid may change shape upon stiffening. Highly domed lids are difficult to fit because they shrink inward. It is better to make lids a bit too big than too small; they can be cut down but not expanded. Pottery lids should fit with a certain amount of play. Allowance must be made for glaze. If the pot or its lid warp slightly, too tight a fit will mean that the lid will go on in only one position. Pot and lid should dry together to minimize warping.

Some potters make lidded pots of only two or three sizes, so that no matter what shape the pots are, the openings and the lid sizes are standardized. This makes the lids more or less interchangeable.

KNOBS

The knob is the terminating accent, the punctuation of the covered pot. The knob may rise up as a perky, upright form, or it may be low, hugging the surface of the lid. Knobs which seem to be right in the bisqued stage may prove to be slippery and hard to hold onto when glazed. As in other details of potting, knobs are made with sufficient boldness and scale to translate well into the shrunken fired state. Instead of thrown knobs, pots may sprout handlelike forms, lugs, straps, or modelled birds, insects, animals, fungi and the like.

ORIENTAL POTS WITH LIDS

Pots with lids were not a common form in the Orient. But some of the greatest lidded pots were made during the ancient Silla period in Korea. In many of these pieces, pot and lid have an equal role in the design. The Japanese favored lacquer lids for pottery, and often these were specially made to fit eccentric openings. In the tea ceremony the harsh and rather grating sound of a pottery lid was considered undesirable and the covered water pot was usually provided with a lacquer lid which produced only a soft muffled sound.

CASSEROLES

The casserole is a popular and useful pottery form. It is always in demand and serves as a bread-and-butter item for many potters. Although the form is simple, the functional requirements of the cooking pot are demanding. In fact, the fulfillment of these practical dictates rather drastically reduces the

121

Fig. 94 Opposite. *Squash.*
Fig. 95 *Throwing a lid on the hump.*
Fig. 96 *The finished lid is cut off the hump.*
Fig. 97 *Making the flange on a lid thrown upside down.*

Fig. 98 Covered jar. The domed lid continues without interrupting the line of the jar, with the knob treated as a pinnacle.
Fig. 99 Covered jar with cap lid.

Fig. 100 Covered jar. The recessed lid settles in securely. Fig. 101 Covered jar. A knob is unnecessary because the overhang makes the lid easy to pick up by the edge.

potter's choices in such matters as shape, proportion, size, and the design of lids and knobs.

The proportion of the casserole is pretty much determined by the facts of cooking. If the piece is too shallow and broad, the contents of the casserole will develop too high a proportion of upper crust, and the food tends to dry out in the oven. If, on the other hand, the piece is too deep, there will not be enough crust in relation to the total content and the dish being cooked will lack the very condition sought after in baking, namely a crusty upper surface covering a moist interior. The indication, then, is for a pot which is horizontal in emphasis but is not too shallow or flat. A lower casserole is much easier to put in and take out of the oven than a more upright shape. The bean pot is something of an exception to this rule. Beans need to cook in a moist condition and come out better if baked in a pot which is about as deep as it is wide, with a relatively small amount of crust forming in relation to the mass.

The interior surface of the casserole needs to be smooth for ease of cleaning. Cleaning baking dishes is hard at best, and roughness, sharp corners or knuckle marks make it harder. The area under the flange especially should be smooth and without a sharp turn.

If the casserole is to have a foot at all, it should be wide in diameter for stability and low to take up little oven space.

The opening is large to facilitate serving the food and to give an ample crust area. Ease of cleaning is a factor here. Also, if the opening is too small, the visual delight of a well-cooked surface of food is lessened.

Since the casserole must be picked up while hot, lugs or handles are provided at the sides. These must be prominent enough to be felt beneath the pot holders.

The lid is best made low. A highly domed lid takes up oven space and gives too much steam space above the food, which causes sogginess. The knob also should be low but of a shape which is easily grasped through the pot holder.

To make for easier cleaning, the flange is better placed on the lid than on the pot.

To forestall breakage from thermal shock, the body of the casserole is best made in a rounded form without sharp corners. In view of this consideration, a form somewhat like a doughnut without a hole is favored.

If too many of these practical matters in the design are overlooked or sacrificed to art, the cooking pot will not be satisfactory in use, however handsome it may be on the shelf. From the above restrictions, one might imagine casserole making to be totally concentrated on function. But as in the case of other pottery forms, subtleties can play within narrow limits, and the full exploitation of form, detail, color, and glaze texture can give ample scope for individual interpretation.

19 CUPS, TEA BOWLS, & MUGS

Of all the needs that potters have ministered to, drinking is perhaps the most basic. The first cup was the two cupped hands, holding water from stream or pond. Before pottery came the halved gourd or coconut shell. Some early pottery pieces in fact seem to have been made in imitation of the gourd.

CUPS

The first pottery cups had some qualities not present in vitrified and glazed ware. They were low-fired, soft, absorbent. The clay surface, with its slight tooth, felt good to the hand and was secure to grasp, not slippery when wet. The lip, finished and smoothed by the fingers, was right for the mouth. The taste and tactile quality of bisqued clay is unlike that of any other material. It is not cold like metal or slimy like wet wood. The damp clay clings to the lips slightly and has a mysterious earthy taste and aroma. Water, kept for a brief time in a soft clay cup, develops a special taste. It is also cooled by evaporation through the sides of the cup.

The cup is such a simple form—just a small cylinder or bowl-like vessel. Its functional aspects are few. The cup works best if the height and width are about the same. The emphasis may be either toward the upright or the horizontal, but if the cup is too high it will be unstable. On the other hand, if it is too broad and low, the contained liquid will slosh and splash. In broad cups, hot liquid will cool too fast. If there is no handle, a foot will make the cup easier to pick up and to hold. The rim touching the lips is smooth and may turn outward slightly but not inward. This edge or rim, if too thick, will feel awkward at the lips. Inside, the cup is smooth, without ridges or sharp corners. The scale is determined by the amount that is comfortable to drink at one time. Since the cups are relatively small, their handles are modest in size and open for no more than one finger.

STEMMED CUPS

The *kylix,* drinking cup of the ancient Greeks, is a shallow dish having a high stemmed foot and two handles. Drinking from it requires a poised attention and the use of both hands. The form seems to indicate that with the Greeks drinking was more ritualistic than with us, involving a controlled gesture. A somewhat comparable shape, used ceremoniously, is the chalice, the stemmed cup used for the wine of holy communion. The word, chalice, derives from the Latin *kalix,* cup.

TEA BOWLS

The development of the cup in China and Japan is intimately connected with tea drinking. Although tea is mentioned in Chinese literature as early as the third century, its widespread popularity as a beverage did not occur until the Tang period, and before this time most Chinese cups seem to have been intended for wine drinking. In the Sung period, bowls intended specifically to be used for green tea were made in the Chien district. Tea was prepared from the powdered leaf by whipping it together with hot water into a thick frothy mixture. To enhance the green color of the tea, a dark-glazed bowl was preferred. The Chien tea bowls, known as *temmoku* by the Japanese, were widely used in China and were especially revered by the Japanese devotees of the tea ceremony. The *temmoku* bowls are rather small and tend toward a conical shape. The foot is very narrow. The bowls are meant to be held in the two hands. The rim is subtly formed with a slight depression which fits the lower lip when drinking.

Tea made by the infusion method, since it is a clear amber or greenish liquid, called for white tea bowls to best display the color. The Chinese porcelain tea bowl, often paper-thin and translucent, has typically a delicate, subtly curved profile. Invariably, it has a foot ring. In use, the fingers are held against the foot, supporting the cup, while the thumbs hold the lip. Held in this way the heat of the cup is not transmitted to the hands, thus making a handle unnecessary.

In Japan the tea bowl has the status of an art form. It is difficult for us to understand how the humble tea bowl could be the object of so much interest and veneration. But for centuries tea drinking and the customs which have grown up around it have been an important aspect of Japanese culture. The bowls used for tea are not merely pots to be bought, used, discarded; they are symbols of nature, time, beauty, feeling, friendship, and hospitality.

Tea was introduced to Japan by Zen Buddhist monks returning from China in the twelfth century. *Temmoku* tea bowls made in Chien were also brought from China at this time. At first, tea was considered primarily medicinal, but it soon became associated with the austerity and meditative practices of the Zen establishments. The potters at Seto tried diligently to copy the Chien tea bowls; in some measure they succeeded. They made tea bowls with dark brown, rather fluid glazes. Tea drinking became formalized into what is known as the tea ceremony during the sixteenth century.

Fig. 102 Opposite. *Raku tea bowl. The form was thrown, but manipulated somewhat by the fingers after throwing.*

Chinese bowls were preferred but were so rare that they were available only to the aristocracy. When the Japanese war-lord Hideoshi invaded Korea in 1592, an important part of the loot taken was Korean pottery and porcelain. Korean potters were also taken as captives and were put to work in Japan, where their superior knowledge of ceramic techniques led to the development of porcelain in the southern island of Kyushu. This adventure of Hideoshi's became known as the "potters war." Although Hideoshi was an iron-willed general and all-powerful ruler, he was fond of the tea ceremony and a patron of potters.

KOREAN RICE BOWLS

Among the imported or commandeered pottery were Korean rice bowls of coarse stoneware. The Japanese valued these highly for the tea ceremony. The rice bowls were made for the peasants and in Korea were thought to be

Fig. 103 Opposite top. *"Winter" tea bowl.*
Fig. 104 Opposite bottom. *"Summer" tea bowl.*
Fig. 105 Below. *Cutting off a bowl. Excess clay has been left at the bottom of the form for trimming the foot.*

valueless. But they had just the rustic quality, and the casual earthy shape demanded by the aesthetic of tea. Understatement, quietness, humility, and limited means were expressed in these bowls. The form is rather open, and the prominent foot is carved out with apparently careless haste. The glazes are full of imperfections such as pits, crazing, and crawls. To fill the demand, Japanese potters made imitations of the Korean bowls, but somehow the devil-may-care style of the originals eluded them.

RAKU TEA BOWLS

A highly original pottery form, the Raku tea bowls appeared in Japan during Hideoshi's time. Their unassuming forms represent the quintessence of the Japanese sensibility and their genius for investing a simple object with an inner mystical spirit. At the time of its development, direct modelling was almost never used for utilitarian pots, and there was no precedent for such a style in either Korea or China. The beauty of the Raku bowl lies in its subtle movement. The clay seems to have grown rather hesitantly from foot to lip and the undulation of the lip makes the circumference into a line with hills and valleys. Of all the world's pots, the Raku bowl is perhaps the most inviting to the touch.

"SUMMER" AND "WINTER" TEA BOWLS

Japanese tea bowls might be divided into two types. The open, rather wide bowl, similar to a rice bowl, is the "summer" tea bowl (Figure 104). Its broad pool of tea cools quickly. The "winter" tea bowl is shaped more like a drum, and its more closed-in form keeps the tea warm (Figures 102, 103, and 106). Although the outside of a tea bowl may be rough, the inside is usually smoothly made and glazed to prevent damage to the bamboo tea whisk used to stir the green tea to a froth. Japanese tea bowls sometimes have a notch cut in the foot. This is a vestigial feature, copied from old rice bowls. These were packed for shipment stacked one nestled into the other with straw between and tied with a cord. The top bowl had a notched foot to secure the string.

THE HANDLED CUP AND SAUCER

The handled tea cup and saucer appeared early in Europe in the seventeenth century. It was perhaps an expression of refinement in manners. Developing etiquette formulated such rules for the table as the use of one hand only for eating, the other hand being kept in the lap. When only one hand is used, the handle on the cup becomes almost a necessity. Cups were

Fig. 106 Opposite. *Raku tea bowl. This piece and the piece in Figure 102 illustrate the effectiveness of glaze in lending interest and warmth to extremely simple and unassuming forms.*

made small, perhaps to make the pouring and passing of tea occur more frequently as a social gesture. Handles were designed for one finger at the most, or more commonly, to be pinched between the forefinger and the thumb. The saucer facilitated passing, part of the ritual of tea. It also caught spills, an important function where tables are covered with fine linens or damask tablecloths.

The saucer is a small plate with a well into which the foot of the cup fits and is prevented from slipping about. The rim of the saucer must be high enough for easy grasp and picking up and to give enough depth to contain any spills. Although the unmannered sometimes pour tea out into them for rapid cooling, saucers were never meant to be drunk from. The cup and saucer must be designed to allow enough room below the handle for one finger.

MUGS

The mug suggests a more hearty and uninhibited way of life than the cup and saucer. Perhaps the pottery mug was originally the poor man's substitute for the metal tankard. Wide bottomed, it resists overturn, and its sturdy substance and shape enable it to be thrown about in taverns, or pounded against the table as a signal for "more." The association of mugs with malt liquor is intimate. It is typified by the German beer stein. The old Rhennish salt-glazed stein with a pewter lid was almost an art form in itself. On its sides were complex decorative schemes which might include landscapes, figures, and events. The pulled handles were highly sculptural and the pop-up metal lids well engineered. For some mysterious reason, beer tastes better in a pottery mug than it does in glass (or from the can).

Old Staffordshire mugs are among the best. They were made for the common man, and had few pretentions toward art or refinement. Beautifully and quickly thrown, their shapes are simple yet strong and the handles are invariably well made. Before the industrial revolution, English potters were masters of handle making.

One might conclude that there is not much to a mug, just a cylinder with a handle. It would seem an easy form for the potter to master. But the form has its subtleties. The cylinder of the mug can be given various distinctive emphases, either barrel-shaped, straight-sided, or convex. The nature of the trimming, the finger marks, the treatment of the lip, and the overall proportion and scale give the potter scope for invention.

The cup, surely thought by most to be a form unworthy of much creative energy, was almost rediscovered by Ron Nagel with his wonderful series of cups made in the 1960s. Some of them did not depart radically from the traditional shape, but others expressed wholly original arrangements of parts. In his hands the cup regained its status as a ceremonial object.

134

20 TEAPOTS

The teapot presents a special challenge for the potter. He must bring a number of parts into relationship and make them work together both functionally and aesthetically. Body, foot, lid, knob, handle, and spout must be brought together into one consistent form.

The teapot can be thought of primarily as a covered jar. The body of the pot and the lid are the dominant elements. The handle and spout, which enable the pot to be picked up and to pour, are supporting or completing features. From this point of view, the pot itself is best made with the attention given first to its volume, to its full realization as a container. The body, especially in view of the appendages it must carry, needs to be a strongly stated form, not meager or hesitant. Unless the body of the pot emerges as a clarified shape, the parts which are added to it can never be assimilated to the total form.

Figure 107 shows the various features of the teapot. The body can have either a horizontal or a vertical emphasis, or it can be something approaching a sphere or a drum. If the porportion of the body is too tall and narrow, it may make the pot teetery, the balance uncertain, and the pouring aim difficult. On the other hand, if the body of the pot is too low and broad, the center of gravity will be too far from the handle and picking up will be made difficult. A proportion in which height and width are not radically different works best. The body, since it must sprout the other parts, is perhaps best kept rather simple in form without an excess of turns, bulges, or corners. The interior, as it moves up toward the opening for the lid, should not have ridges or angles on the inside which would interfere with emptying.

The foot is usually not a prominent feature of the teapot. It may be eliminated. Too much foot means additional weight and perhaps an element of instability. If there is a foot, it should be sufficiently wide to prevent teetering. Visually, even a modest foot can give a feeling of lightness and can emphasize the springing curve at the base of the pot.

The opening and lid establish the character of the upper part of the form. The opening is made wide enough for easy draining. Since the used tea

135

leaves must be flushed out through the top, a small opening, even though it may look well, will prove to be a nuisance. The lid is made to seat firmly so it will not fall out even when the pot is tilted for total emptying of the tea through the spout. A recessed lid, or a lid with a deep flange extending somewhat down into the opening is better than a flat lid which fits into a flange in the opening. Some teapots are provided with a locking device in the form of a lug which fits under the flange, but this is not really necessary. If the pot is to have an overhead handle, the lid and knob will need to be low to allow room for putting on and taking off. Teapots usually have a lid with a knob, but if the edge of the lid projects a bit it can be lifted off perfectly well without a knob.

The handle is attached at a comfortable position on the body and usually rises at least to the level of the lid. Handles which rise rather sharply at the shoulder work well. The handle clings fairly close to the body, keeping the hand near the center of weight. A somewhat straplike handle gives a secure grip free from wobble.

The spout need be only long enough to give a well-directed stream of tea into the cup. Usually it protrudes no more than about one half of the diameter of the body of the pot. It can either be a tapering or a tubelike form. Excessive taper, that is a very wide base narrowing down to a small opening, may create turbulence in the liquid and cause gurgling. The inside of the

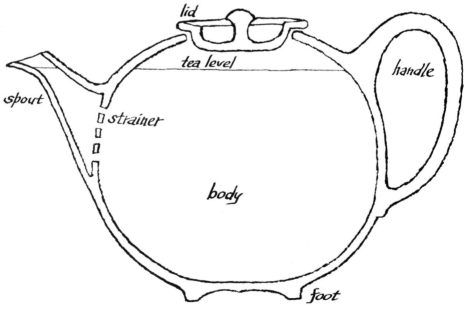

Fig. 107   Features of the teapot.

spout needs to be at least as large as the diameter of, say, a fountain pen and it can be bigger than that and still pour well. It should be smooth inside, without constrictions. At the end, the spout will terminate in a sharp lip which cuts off the flow of tea and prevents dripping. The direction of the spout at this point should be roughly parallel to the table; then, when the pot is tilted, the area just under the edge of the lip of the spout will be uphill to the tea. A feature which helps to prevent dribbling is a little ditch or channel cut on the inside of the spout beginning at the very edge or lip and running back a bit into the spout. When the pour is cut off, the tea tends to run back down this little groove instead of down the outside of the spout. Another factor influencing the pour is the design of the strainer. Traditionally, the strainer has seven holes, perhaps because six circles arranged around a central circle makes all of the circles tangent. But seven strainer holes are a bare minimum; nine or twelve holes arranged in rows are better. More holes allow the tea to flow through the strainer without restriction or turbulence. Turbulence is lessened if the clay wall of the pot is thinned at the area of the strainer.

The position of the spout is arranged so that when the pot is reasonably full the tea level does not come above the end of the spout.

The teapot handle is usually attached to the side, opposite the spout. Another possibility is the handle which is positioned above like a bail (Figure 109). A pot with this kind of handle is easy to pick up and to pour from. But the presence of the overhead handle interferes somewhat with access to the lid.

A bail handle made of raffia, bamboo, reed, or wire can be attached to lugs at the top of the pot (Figure 111). When not in use, the bail drops to the side of the pot and does not interfere with the lid. The bail gives a tendency for the pot to waggle from side to side a little during pouring. Another type of handle is the side handle, a protruding lug (Figure 114). This works quite well on small teapots, but for larger ones, the grip is not secure enough. If the handle is put on the left side of the pot, it will function well only for right-handed people. It will be seen that all of these handle solutions have their advantages and disadvantages.

If the functional requirements for the teapot as outlined above are faithfully met it would seem that there is a very narrow space left for variation, or for the establishment of some unique form. It is obvious that many great teapots do not attain the ultimate in efficiency, while others may break all the rules and still make it as a pot. As with all other traditional pottery forms, the generalized shape is to some degree established by function, but variations and interpretations may bring it to life. Function sets the stage and creates the limits within which the energies and insights of the potter can work. The ground rules of teapot-making as I have given them might pre-

Fig. 108 Making a teapot spout.

vent one from making a really bad teapot, but it should be understood that they would never by themselves enable one to make a really good one.

FIRST STEPS

The body of the teapot and the lid are made first, establishing the basis of the design. It is important that the walls of the pot be thin and light. If necessary, the pot can be shaved down rather drastically after it has stiffened. To trim the body upside down, a chum may be necessary to prevent injury to the detail of the opening. It is advisable to make several lids for each body. It only takes a few minutes to make a lid and to have a selection from which the best can be chosen helps in achieving a good scale and fit.

Spouts also are quickly made and extras improve the chances of a good marriage between body and spout. Made from the hump, the spout is alternately drawn up and collared in until it is the right size and shape (Figure 108). It is always made longer than the final spout so it can be cut and adapted to the body. When the spout has stiffened, it is reamed out from the back to make it thin and smooth on the interior and is then cut to fit the pot and to tilt at the right angle. The strainer holes are cut in the pot by punching out the clay with the sharpened end of a potter's knife or with the angled and sharpened end of a small copper tube. The wall of the pot at the strainer is shaved thinner and the edges of the holes made sharp and unobstructed.

When the spout is attached, it can either be made to appear as a separate but joined form, or the transition from spout to body can be smoothed out so the spout will appear to grow without interruption from the body. Since a hand-made spout is actually a form which is made separately, perhaps it is better to accept frankly the articulation between it and the body.

With the spout attached and the lid on, the scale and placement of the handle can be visualized. So much work has gone into the teapot by this time that the potter may be nervous about the handle. But if it's not right the first time, it can always be cut off and done over.

Teapots have a rather odd character. There is something slightly anthropomorphic about them. They are balanced and rather squatty, but the spout and handle stretching out into space can give a certain liveliness and animation.

In spite of the fact that tea originated in the Orient, the teapot as we know it is not found in classic Chinese or Japanese pottery. The Chinese and the Koreans made wine ewers which are quite similar to teapots and it is possible that the latter was first created as an imitation of these pouring vessels. Teapots were little used in China or Japan because there tea is made differently from the Western manner. Frothy green tea is made by pouring hot water directly over powdered leaves in the cup. When tea is brewed, only a small amount is made at a time and the tea is not allowed to steep more than

Fig. 109 Top. Teapot with overhead bail. The spout is long and pipelike, and its joint with the body is not smoothed over.

Fig. 110 Middle. Teapot. The rather upright form calls for the long spout, which was made by rolling clay on a wooden brush handle.

Fig. 111 Bottom. Teapot. The lugs will take a bamboo bail. Lids without knobs are good on teapots with overhead bails because they take up less room.

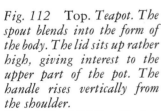

Fig. 112 Top. Teapot. The
spout blends into the form of
the body. The lid sits up rather
high, giving interest to the
upper part of the pot. The
handle rises vertically from
the shoulder.

Fig. 113 Middle. Teapot.
The recessed knob does not
interrupt the ovoid form of the
body. The joint between the
spout and the body is distinct.

Fig. 114 Bottom. Teapot
with side handle.

a few minutes. Therefore, smaller pots which hold only a cup or two are used. These pots have large openings, so the mass of leaves can be easily dumped out, and small spouts. For Europeans, this method of making tea was time-consuming and used up too much tea. It also produced lukewarm tea, which is acceptable to the Japanese but is anathema to Westerners. The teapot thus took the form of a vessel which would hold a quantity of tea, six cups or more, and keep it hot. The spout was designed to pour well and accurately into a cup which was left on the table rather than being held in the hands.

The teapot reached its fullest development in England where teapots became revered objects in every home. Few good English wheel-made teapots exist, however. This is because tea drinking became popular around 1750, when the potteries were being converted to molded production, so most of the teapots were cast or pressed. Many English teapots were made in fanciful forms, sometimes in the image of birds or animals. A popular idea was to have a teapot created which was actually a model of the owner's house, with handle and spout added. Handles were sometimes made of ropes of clay twisted together, or made to resemble vines or twigs.

The teapot may be now on the verge of obsolescence. Brewing tea in a pot has been largely replaced by use of the tea bag. And gatherings of five or six people who are all inclined to take tea together seem to be becoming rare.

21 ALTERING & COMBINING THROWN FORMS

The thrown pot, even though it may assume an infinite number of shapes, always circles about an axis and is more or less symmetrical. This circularity and symmetry, this limitation of the form to variation in one dimension only, relates all wheel-made pots to each other, joins them into one family. Thrown pots, because of their symmetry, tend to be quiet, unassertive, and easy to approach.

The limitations imposed by the wheel are usually accepted by potters as being a built-in feature of their craft. Some may chafe under the restrictions of throwing and turn with relief to hand building and to sculpture. Others find comfort in wheel work, finding that it protects them from having to make the endless choices involved in free form; on the wheel, at least, one formal aspect of the work is dictated by the process. The wheel furnishes a constant, a framework which, by narrowing the possibilities, provides some security.

The practice of altering thrown forms opens up an area of pottery design somewhere between the formality of the wheel and the total freedom of modeling. The unique character of a wheel-made pot can be varied and enlarged upon by moving the clay away from its position around the vertical axis or by distortions which break its regularity and symmetry.

All pots are not born perfectly symmetrical, and one class of altered pots might be those which, deliberately or not, were made with a drift away from that regularity which is normal to skilled throwing. Rims may waver up and down, sides bulge, and openings go oblong instead of round. Or twists may result from the stresses of inept throwing. When such irregularities are the result of a lack of skill, they usually contribute little of value to the final expression. But it must be recognized that some of the greatest pots in the world are crooked. In Japan, distorted and lopsided pots which have been pushed out of their original thrown state are part of an old tradition. This tradition, the acceptance and love of asymmetrical pots, seems to have come about

Fig. 115   Overleaf, left. *Indenting the side of a freshly thrown bottle.*
Fig. 116   Overleaf, right. *Bottle. Alternating round and elongated dents break into the form.*

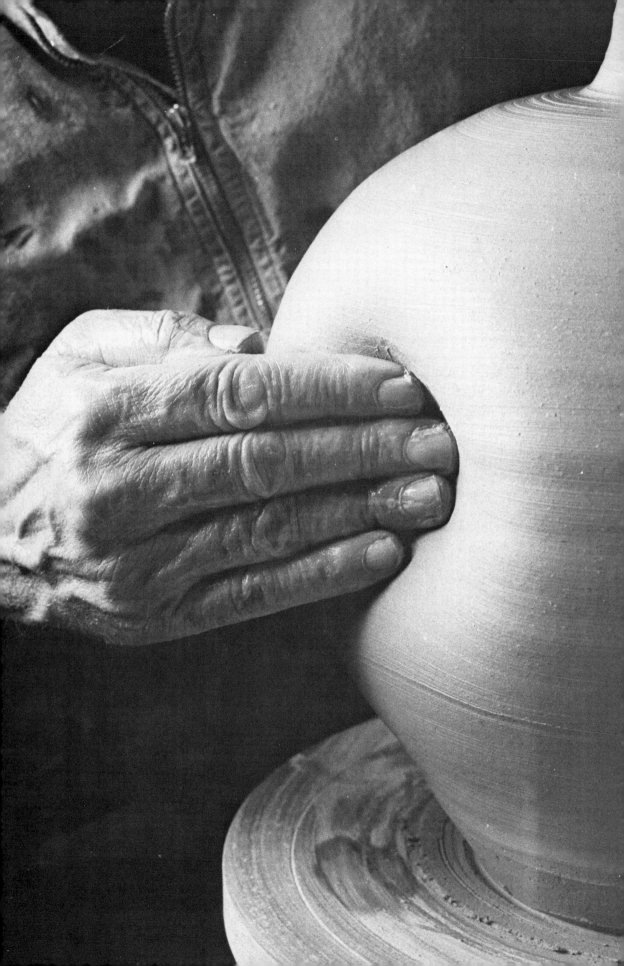

Fig. 117 Top. *Using a wooden tool to make a dent.*
Fig. 118 Bottom. *A deliberate break, patched from the inside.*

partly as a result of the fact that early Japanese throwing techniques made crookedness the rule rather than the exception. Pots were made on light, slow turning wheels and were commonly built up with coils and finished by throwing as described in the previous section. Storage jars and other pieces made at Seto, Shigaraki, Bizen, and Tamba from the twelfth century on were almost invariably off-center to some degree; in some cases they were dramatically lopsided. It is doubtful if this crookedness originally had any aesthetic justification. It was just the way the pots naturally took form, given the material, the process, and the working attitudes of the potters. They were making utilitarian pieces for an agricultural and rural market where smoothness, neatness, and regularity of form were in no way essential for the successful function of the pots. But although these pots had a humble origin and were meant for seed storage, pickling, or the collection of offal, they have a noble style. Their forms are vigorous, strong, and generous. Their crookedness seems to be an integral part of their character and reinforces a sense of vitality. The moving, organic quality of these old pots is also amplified by the uneven and varied glazing and flashing which occurred during firing in primitive wood burning kilns. More is said about these glazes in section 26.

Fig. 119 Distorting a freshly thrown bowl.
Fig. 120 Overleaf, left. The upper part of this piece consists of the collapsed and torn remains of another thrown piece.
Fig. 121 Overleaf, right. Altered thrown pot. The sides have been dented in and the rim torn and rolled back.

Fig. 123 Combined form. The upper part, given welts by pressure of the fingers from within, was thrown upside down from its present position. The top was completed by pinching and extending the thick clay, which had been at the bottom.

Fig. 124   Combined form. The middle section consists of slabs added to the thrown lower part. The upper part was made by combining fragments of other thrown pieces.

Fig. 125   Tall bottle. Three thrown forms are incorporated, giving a complex profile and a variety of textures and striations.

in the history of pottery for this drama are few, because traditionally potters have worked for the completion and affirmation of form, and for abstract balance and stability.

Altering thrown pots and playing with their yielding form can easily be overdone. At some point the original piece is fatally wounded, fallen victim to a pervading softness, mushiness, and sense of collapse. As in other forms of expression, total freedom from the constraints of formal relationships may lead merely to chaos. Things made of clay always hover on the edge of caving in anyway, at least when they are fresh and very soft. Manipulations which tend toward the erosion of the pot's basic structure may produce an effect of weakness, of hesitancy.

One of the unique things about clay-working is the ease with which parts can be joined. Merely push two clay forms together with some slip between and they will be permanently attached and are in truth one. The making of combines, assemblages, and constructions is therefore a very logical ap-

Fig. 126 Opposite. *Combined form.*
Fig. 127 Below. *Breasts.*

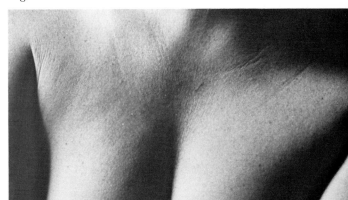

proach to take with clay. I discussed earlier the methods of joining parts to produce a larger whole, but there is also the possibility of assembling whole or partially thrown pieces where each part retains a degree of identity. The teapot with a thrown spout and lid is a practical example of this, but an infinite number of forms can be made having perhaps little functional orientation. Tall pots can be made by piling shorter ones on top of each other, or pots may cluster into agglomerations (Figures 125 and 126). The rounded volumes and the fingered striations of thrown pots may then become only one of the contributing elements in a new composition. Combinations of thrown and slab-made parts offer the possibility of contrasts between the flat and the rounded, the straight and the curved (Figure 124).

Fig. 128   Cut form.

22 HAND BUILT POTTERY

The techniques of hand building with clay are essentially simple and easily mastered. Since clay is pliable, plastic, and stays where it is put and since it may be added to and extended, there are no great obstacles to be overcome in making a pot by hand.

There are three basic methods of hand building. The first is to make the whole piece from one lump of clay by pinching and extending it. Another is to build up the form gradually by the addition of wads or gobs which are smoothed and shaped as the work progresses. The third way is to develop the piece by assembling or adding preformed coils or slabs.

DIRECT MODELING OR PINCHING

Modeling a pot directly from one ball of clay by pinching and squeezing is certainly the most basic pottery technique. It requires no tools or equipment, and the potter is in direct contact through his hands with the thing he is making.

To pinch a bowl, the round ball is gradually formed into a hollow by pressure from the thumbs. At first the shape resembles a worn-out tennis ball pushed in from one side. Then the sides of the hollow are gradually thinned and extended by numerous pinching or squeezing pressures between the thumbs and the fingers. If a symmetrical form is desired, the pinching is carried out rhythmically as the bowl is turned, and care is taken not to thin one area more than others. The whole bowl is allowed to grow and take shape in an all-over way. Bowls made in this way tend to be rather open and flat because as the pinching proceeds the rim becomes ever more widely stretched (Figure 129). If a deep bowl is desired, the rim can be allowed to dry a bit while the sides and bottom of the bowl are covered with plastic or cloth to keep the clay soft. Then, when work resumes, the rim, slightly stiffened, tends to hold its diameter while the sides and the bottom are being expanded. In the process the rim inevitably gets somewhat crooked, but this irregularity can be trimmed off if desired.

The scale of pinched pots is rather limited by the length of the fingers.

159

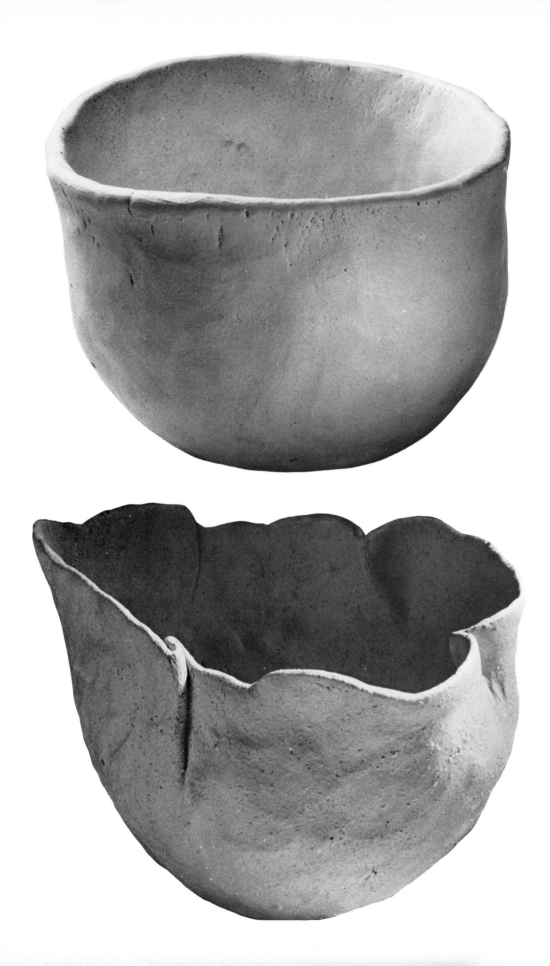

Larger shapes can be made by using one hand inside like an anvil and pressing or beating on the outside with the other. Careful management of the clay is necessary, with pauses allowed to dry the rim if it is to be kept narrow.

Another way to make a larger piece by pinching is to work on a ball of clay first from one side, pinching it up into a pot, leaving half of the ball as a solid hemisphere. This solid half is then pinched and extended in the same way. With the fingers and paddle, the clay is coaxed over the opening of the second half to form the bottom of the pot.

Pinch pots can be made in the form of cylinders, bowls, plates, cups, globular vases, or completely enclosed spheres. Irregular forms can be made which combine the elements of several geometric shapes. Intricately varied wrinkles, mounds and valleys, protuberances and the like add complexity and interest to the pinched pot.

Fig. 129   Opposite top. *Bowl pinched from one lump of clay.*
Fig. 130   Opposite bottom. *Bowl pinched from one lump of clay.*
Fig. 131   Below. *Hand-built tea bowls. The forms were pinched up from added wads. The feet were added after the bowls had stiffened; a banding wheel was used for rough trimming.*

Pots made by pinching tend to have a soft, irregular quality, a kind of tremulousness and uncertainty. The feeling of the original ball of clay persists into the finished piece. The surface, unless it is scraped off or beaten with a paddle, will ripple slightly from the marks of the fingers. Symmetry about an axis, since it does not come naturally by this method, may seem forced and stiff if it is achieved and the pinched pot which is "perfect," that is round, even, and straight across the top, may have more the look of a carefully prepared model for molded production than a handmade thing.

Paradoxically, pinch pots tend to look somewhat alike (in the same way that thrown pots look alike), no matter who does them. This is not necessar-

Fig. 132   Opposite. *Bowl with foot. Pinched from one lump of clay, with clay crumbs added for texture.*
Fig. 133   Below. *Bowl. Pinched from one lump of clay, with foot added. The form results from pinching the clay between the fingers.*

Fig. 138   Opposite top. *Tomato.*
Fig. 139   Opposite bottom. *Hand-built vase form.*
Fig. 140   Top. *Hand-built vase form.*
Fig. 141   Bottom. *Pepper.*

cussed. The inherent slowness of direct hand building can have a positive rather than a negative value. It enables the potter to let his feelings catch up with his productivity. It directs his attention to the pot as well as to the process. It allows form to ripen and to mature and for the nature of the clay to make itself felt.

The Raku tea bowls of Japan are the only renowned pottery forms which owe their quality to pinching as a method of production. The story of these curious bowls has often been told. Their significance as a cup form and a tea ceremony utensil was discussed in section 20 on cups and tea bowls. They are quite unique in the history of pottery, and it is significant that such little black or brown bowls, modest in size and unremarkable in color, could so excite the admiration and veneration of generations of Japanese art lovers. They were inherently modest, made just for tea. Their forms were arrived at not by design, or by conscious willing or forcing of a shape into the reality of the third dimension, but by feeling.

It may be true that the prototypes for the Raku bowls were made by Korean roof-tile makers who did not know how to use the potter's wheel and therefore resorted to pinching and modeling. This does not matter. What matters is the living quality of the form, and its sensitive relation both to the maker and to the user. In fact, to handle one of these bowls and to feel the undulating form and the slightly rising and falling lip is to almost feel that one has created the bowl oneself. It is a very different sensation than the encounter with classical Chinese pottery, which stands in a kind of self-created halo, a presence made somewhat impenetrable by its poise and perfection. I am not trying to compare Chinese work unfavorably with Japanese here, only to point out that pottery can include these very different impulses, these different concepts of form. We should not forget that the Raku bowl, although its modest form seems to speak only of clay and tea, is actually part of a spiritual process, a distinct way of life. This way of tea had, for its devotees, implications which seeped into every aspect of life. Its basis is Zen, and the realization that everything one does counts and that life is for here and now rather than for some unimaginable denouement in the future opened the way for an appreciation of the quiet quality of a simple clay cup which one held in the two hands, contemplating the frothy green tea inside. The pot, too, can be a mirror, only awaiting the polish of one's spirit.

COIL BUILDING

There are two ways to make coils out of plastic clay. One is to roll a piece of clay on the table with the palms and fingers of the hand, gradually extending it to the desired length and diameter (Figure 135). It is best to use some rather absorbent surface to keep the clay from sticking; a cloth stretched over a wooden table is ideal. The coils have a troublesome habit of

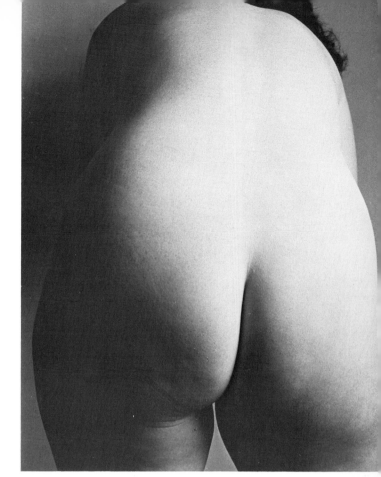

Fig. 142   Back.

going flat. This can be prevented by letting the coil roll free after each rolling motion so the fingers make a renewed contact on the roll. These ropes of clay can be made up ahead of time in sufficient number to make the whole pot and kept damp and soft until ready for use. A quicker way to make coils is to form them from a lump of clay held between the palms (Figure 136). The clay is rolled back and forth and squeezed, mostly between the heels of the two hands. Hopefully a coil will develop which will extend downward in increasing length as the rolling proceeds. It is difficult to make very small or very even coils this way, but it is fast. The Pueblo women potters in the southwestern United States invariably make coils by this method.

In some ways, building with these ropes or coils of clay seems a rather awkward method. The unit involved is so small in diameter that to build up a wall requires a great many joinings, and these joints must either be incorporated as part of the design or must be laboriously obliterated by modeling or scraping. Moreover, the presence of innumerable joints in a piece invites cracking in drying and firing, and unless the joining is carefully and skillfully done the pot will surely be lost. The usual method is to start with a modeled or beaten-out disk for the bottom of the piece and to lay one coil on another, welding and joining, until the pot takes shape. To work well and join well, the coils have to be quite soft, therefore, after a few coils are in place, time must be taken for drying to prevent the distortion or collapse of the piece.

23 FORMS MADE BY COMPRESSION & DRAPING

In throwing, and to a lesser extent in modeling, pinching, or coiling, the forces which shape the piece come mostly from the inside. These forces, analogous in a sense to the content or charge of the form, press outward and stretch the clay, determining the quality of the shape. Constricting, inward-tending forces, such as collaring in or squeezing, act as a counterpoint and serve to limit or terminate expansion.

But pots can also be formed largely or entirely by pressure from the outside, and pieces made this way have a distinctive character. For example, as noted in section 10, pots can be made by throwing and then beaten, paddled, or dented from the outside. Such pieces will gain a certain feeling of compaction, or density. Flattened places speak of the flattening effect of an outside force. Paddling can eliminate throwing marks and other undulations of form and replace them with a smooth, hammered surface.

COMPRESSION

A method is presented here for making pots entirely through external pressure. A ball of clay is wedged up equal in volume to the intended finished pot. This ball can be slightly stiffer than the usual consistency for throwing. The mass of clay is then shaped by forceful beating, slapping, rolling, or punching with broad wooden tools, or with rocks, pipes or textured objects. The emergence of the form and the surface texture takes place simultaneously. Since the mass of clay is solid, much greater force can be applied to it than would be possible with hollow forms, so the effect of beating will be quite different from paddling a thrown shape. When the mass of clay has taken on a shape and external texture deemed to be final, it is allowed to dry until the clay stiffens. It is then cut in two with the wire, hollowed out with wire modeling tools, and the two halves recombined with slip. By careful excavation, the walls can be made as thin as desired. A pot made in this way is essentially sculptural in that it originates as a solid mass. Its character is wholly achieved by compaction (Figures 156, 159, 160, and 161).

Fig. 155 *Compression form. Some of the texture results from beating with a textured paddle.*

Fig. 156 *Compression form. Made by beating together separate lumps of clay.*

Fig. 160 Opposite. *Compression form.*
Fig. 161 Below. *Compression form. The striations were the result of beating with a large wooden club.*
Fig. 162 Overleaf left. *Draped form. Slabs of clay were applied to a foam rubber core, allowing overlaps.*
Fig. 163 Overleaf right. *Draped form. Fiberglass cloth saturated with slip was draped over a foam rubber core.*

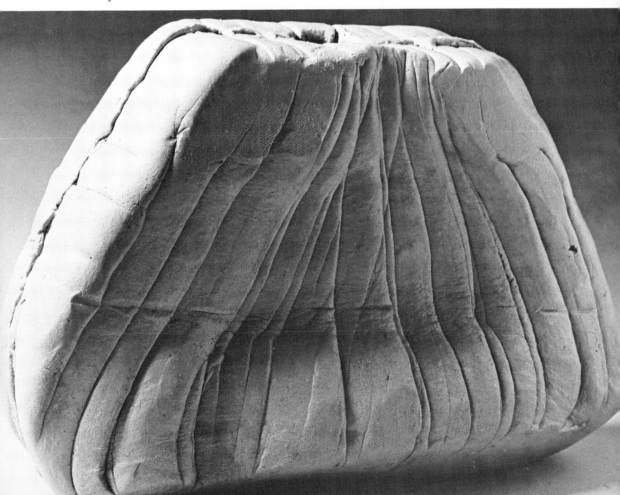

the age-old craft of clay working is of interest. (See Rhodes, *Clay and Glazes for the Potter,* for a description of the process of using fiberglass with clay.)

The draped clay piece in Figure 163 was made by first establishing the form with a foam-rubber core. The rubber was cut, shaped, and fastened onto a light armature of wood. Then the sheets of fiberglass cloth and clay slip were laid over the core, until several thicknesses had been built up to give the desired strength. When drying shrinkage occurs, the clay squeezes in on the soft rubber core, and the reinforcing in the clay gives it sufficient toughness to prevent cracking. The foam rubber and armature burn and disappear during firing.

Pieces made in this way can have a feeling of looseness or flow in the form which is quite different from the effect of compaction in beaten pots or of distention in thrown pots. It is also radically different from the sometimes stiff, boxy quality of the slab construction. Each method, each approach to shaping and moving clay brings about a characteristic image.

24 SOME EXTINCT POTTERY FORMS

Pottery forms have long histories. The basic shape such as bowls, plates, jugs, and storage jars have been persistent, enduring, and they are still with us today.

But there are some forms which have become obsolete and are no longer made. The small number of these extinct pottery forms indicates the universal and relatively unchanging character of pottery.

Oil Lamps: The pottery oil lamp was in widespread use in the ancient world, and old ones are to be found in all of the countries of the Mediterranean. The typical shape is a rather shallow saucer, with a small pulled spout. Sometimes there is a handle opposite this. The oil was placed in the dish, and a wick laid in the oil. The wick crossed the spout, where it burned. When the wick burned down a bit it was pulled out. These oil lamps must have been fire hazards, because when spilled the whole dish of oil could ignite.

Bed Warmers: These are the precursors of the hot-water bottle. They were usually bottle-shaped with the hole in the side rather than at the end. Potted rather thickly in stoneware, the bottle would retain for a long time the heat of the boiling water inside. The bed warmer, wrapped up in a flannel cloth and placed under the covers near the foot of the bed, was a great comfort on cold nights.

Wash-stand Sets: These consisted of a large bowl for washing and a pitcher of about one gallon capacity for water. These sets were very common household items before the advent of running water.

Moustache Cup: A bar just inside the cup on the drinking side is supposed to keep the moustache from drooping into the cup. This design has been revived in the 1970s.

Spinning Weights: These are small clay lemon-shaped pottery weights with a hole for the thread. They were extensively used throughout pre-Columbian America for spinning thread. These weights are sometimes solid, and are usually decorated.

Water Dropper: This form was, and to some extent still is, used in the Orient to add water drop by drop to the ink used in calligraphy and Sumie painting. The form is enclosed and has a tiny hole where the water drips out, and another hole which is covered by the thumb to control the air going into the dropper and thus the rate of flow. The water dropper was made in many forms, sometimes a little box made from slabs, sometimes in the form of fanciful animals or figures. They are often of porcelain.

Tripod Cooker: In prehistoric China, a pottery form was made which had three hollow feet coming down to points. This was presumably made to sit in a fire or bed of charcoal; it would have more stability than a bowl with a rounded bottom.

Beehive Cover: These were in use in Persia until recent times. The entrance to the beehive is covered with a pottery disk about eight inches in diameter. In the center of the disk is a hole for the bees to go in and out. The disks were lavishly decorated in underglaze colors, and were thought to bring success and productivity to the hive.

Toilet Jar: In Japan, the privy—usually inside the house—includes a large pottery jar which receives the waste; this is later pumped or dipped out and taken to the fields for fertilizer. Such jars are still in use in the 1970s, but they are no longer made or installed. Production of these jars, which usually held 30 to 50 gallons, was a mainstay of some potteries.

Soup Tureen: A large and rather deep bowl with a high cover. These impressive pieces were formerly a part of every formal dinner setting. They have become obsolete because present day menus seldom call for quantities of soup, and storage space for such large pieces is scarce.

Gravy Boat: A pouring vessel with attached saucer. This form is still available but is seldom used.

Churn: When butter was made at home, pottery was the ideal material for the churn. It was easily cleaned, impervious and sanitary. Until about 1900, the ceramic churn took the form of a high covered jar with a hole in the lid for the agitator.

Pillow: Ceramic pillows were common in China, Korea, and Japan. Clay seems an unlikely material for a pillow—too hard and cold! Nevertheless, people slept on them. They were usually slab-built in the form of a low box with slanting top surface, and were often lavishly decorated.

25 CLAY & GLAZES

The art of pottery is close to the earth. The clay comes from the earth, is earth. It is tempered with sands, or ground earthy minerals. Water brings it to plasticity. The kiln began as a pocket in the earth, later evolved into a cave in the earth. The fragments of broken pots return to the earth where they persist as inconspicuously as pebbles or clods.

Raw clay relates to mud, to pond bottoms, to compost, to slippery paths, to the silts at the banks of rivers, to dust and to exposed, crumbly cliffs.

Fired, the clay relates to those hard and seemingly unchanging masses which make up mountains: sandstones, shales, granites, basalts, all dense and mottled or colored with a thousand shades of red, brown, grey, pink, and black. Fired clay is, in essence, rock.

Potters learn to respect the clay. They respect its temperament in the raw and its self-assumed transformations in color, hardness, and texture when fired. To make pottery is to work *with* clay. The destiny of potter's clay, to be formed into a pot, to be dried, and to be fired into permanence, requires the collaboration rather than the dominance of the potter. He must respect the need of clay to be gently urged rather than rammed into shape; respect its need for slow drying and careful firing.

EARTHENWARE

Different clays seem to call forth different forms. The soft, absorbent, earthy, and sometimes rough texture of earthenware clay finds expression in rather heavy pottery, with substantial rims and sturdy, wide bottoms. Its fragility makes the overly thin wall a hazard. Yet, some primitive pots are amazingly light and thin. Perhaps the routines of their use were as delicate and gentle as the coil building methods of the potters, and breakage was not a problem. In a culture which does not use furniture but accomplishes cooking and eating on the floor or on the ground, the breakage of pots is minimized.

STONEWARE

The color and texture of fired stoneware indicates hardness, durability, a certain brittleness, density, strength. There is a lessened distinction between the body and the glaze of the pot. Forms for stoneware move toward the rugged, bold, and vigorous. The toothy brown substance of the clay suggests vulcanism, and the tempering of material by fire. Broad treatments of form—generous lips and rims, handles pulled and applied with swiftness and dexterity making neating up and reworking unnecessary, trimming which leaves the mark of the tool, throwing marks, fingered or squeezed knobs, paddlings or distortions of the circle—all of these seem appropriate in stoneware. Pots may be substantial, but the density of the material makes the too-thick pot a dead weight in the hands.

PORCELAIN

Porcelain, approaching glass in its substance, seems to call for a still different range of form. Thinness is required to make use of the clay's translucency. This thinness of wall leads to an overall delicacy of form. Lips and rims are sharp. Appendages, harder to make in porcelain than in the more plastic stoneware or earthenware, tend to be restrained and attached with care and precision. Surfaces are smooth, reflecting the total lack of grog or tooth in the clay. To prevent slumping in the fire, extremes of form are avoided. The rather nonplastic quality of the clay imposes a certain restraint on the thrower, and in contrast to the exuberance of stoneware forms, porcelain is usually compact, rounded, simplified, and inward-turning. Glaze and body become almost as one, and the glassiness dominates over the earthy quality of fired clay. Smoothness, gloss, and the attendant highlighting of forms, lightness, and simplicity are qualities of porcelain which emerge naturally from a sensitive handling of the material. Lightness or whiteness of color has the meaning in ceramics of the refinement of the material until all traces of iron or other dark minerals are removed, leaving the pure, essential, clay substance. Historically, the last important technical development of pottery, porcelain, in its purity and simplicity can be thought of as an ultimate refinement.

GLAZES

Pottery existed long before the invention of glaze. The vast achievements of pre-Columbian potters in America were entirely expressed in vessels and figures finished as clay, decorated with colored clay, or textured in the clay surface. Nothing approaching glaze appeared in all of those innumerable primitive potteries made for millennia the world over. Pottery was a clay form, its surface and its substance one and the same.

With the advent of glaze, first employed by the Egyptians about 2000 B.C. or earlier, the focus of attention in pottery turned from the clay form toward the surface and its color, texture, and modulations. The glazed pot, however, even though it was invented so early in history, remained for long a rarity. Glazing was a specialized technique with the Egyptians, and it was not until toward the beginning of the Christian era that glazed pots became common in the Middle East and in China.

With the development of glaze, the pot lost a certain simplicity and directness. It was no longer a primordial earth form. It became a form clothed in another material. Glaze, as distinct from clay, is glassy, smooth, shiny, and colored—actually quite different as a substance. The marriage of these two substances, clay and glazes, has been enduring and successful. But from one point of view, the pot alone, with its integral surface and essentially earthy nature must be considered primal, and the additions to its surface can be seen as a diversion, a complication and a variation sometimes leading to a weakening and diffusion of the pot as a thing in itself.

On the other hand, glazes, and the colors, decorative ways, pictorialism, textures, and refinements that developed from glazes over the centuries, have enriched the art of pottery immeasurably. Each culture, each geographical area, has contributed its interpretation of the potential of glaze and decoration on pottery. Pottery as an art has been deepened and extended by greater variety and scope in surface. Consider how different glaze surfaces can be, not only in method and materials but in spirit and aesthetic: the Rhineland salt-glazed mug and the Japanese ceremonial tea bowl are both glazed drinking vessels! The first is intensely pictorial with its decoration in low relief under a thin, revealing glaze. We feel the sharp, concentrated working of the clay, intricately molded with every detail picked up by the pool of glaze. The Japanese bowl on the other hand is softly formed, gentle in its proportions and shaping, and the glaze wraps it as inconspicuously as frost does a pumpkin. Glazing has been used in countless different ways, sometimes as a means of achieving intricate decorative patterns in subtly related colors, as in Islamic pottery, sometimes to achieve bold, singing monochromatic effects, as in the Ching pottery of China, where a jar may become almost alive because of its intense, even, yet somehow incredible color of yellow, blue, or green.

In Egypt, glazes apparently first came into use because of their potential for color and decorative pattern. The advent of glaze also had the practical effect of making pottery more impervious to liquids, a matter of great importance in the storing of food and pharmaceuticals and in cooking. With glaze, pottery was easier to clean and more sanitary. There is a theory that the widespread use of glazed pots in Europe, replacing wooden or unglazed clay plates and bowls, helped to bring an end to the devastating plagues and epidemics of the Middle Ages. The glazed food containers were less apt to harbor germs. This boon was no doubt somewhat offset by the incidence of lead poisoning which must have occurred to some degree as a result of the

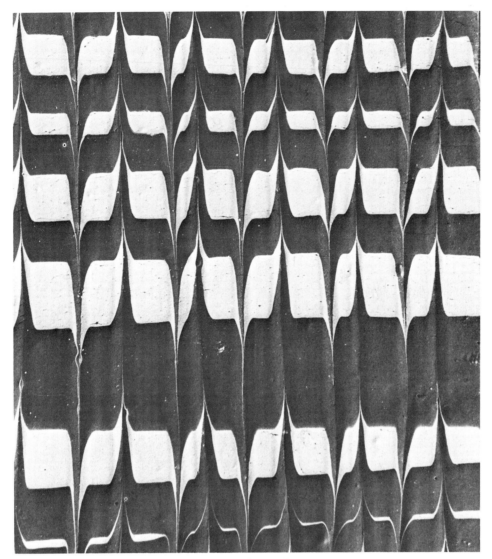

Fig. 164 Slip combing.

use of low-fired, high-lead glazes. But since the awareness of lead poisoning is recent, little is known of its occurrence in former times.

In China, the invention of glaze may have come about through observation of the glazing effects of ash dusts alighting on the posts during firing. When kilns are fired to high temperatures with wood as a fuel, this self-glazing effect, far from being a rare phenomenon, is actually hard to prevent, and unless the pots are placed in protective boxes, or saggers, they are almost sure to show some trace of glaze, at least on the rims or shoulders. It was a simple step from observing the fact that ash caused glaze when it settled on a pot during firing, to actually applying some ash (mixed with a little clay to make it stick) to the surface of the pot before firing.

Some of the pots from China and Japan which were glazed through the firing process, rather than by glaze application, are among the most beautiful glazed pieces in existence. The glaze usually coated only certain parts of the pot, and where it was thick ran down in rivulets. It seemed to have a life of its own. In color, in texture, and in gradations of thickness and tonality, such glazes have a natural and unforced quality, clothing the pot rather than blanketing it. Beside them, most glazed pots appear to be made up of two distinct substances, clay *and* glaze, rather than being a unified whole in which there is little distinction between the substance of the pot and its surface.

This quality of union or identification between the pot and its surface is a matter which will always concern potters. It must be solved anew as the preferences and instincts of each person take form in pottery-making. To some extent the problem seems to solve itself in stoneware, because there the body and the glaze interact with each other in a fusion which gives to the glaze something of the quality of clay and which causes the body to vitrify and turn toward the glassy. The body may give up some of its iron to the glaze, causing spotting, blushes, mottling, or roughness (Figure 170). Fire acts as a leveler, and the stoneware pot is subjected to enough heat to start it toward that ultimate fusion, which, if it were allowed to occur, would result in a melted puddle in which the pot, body, and glaze alike would be dissolved. In porcelain also, the quality of clay and of glaze come naturally towards identification. The glaze is in effect more a glistening or polishing of the body than an obvious addition to it.

In earthware, glaze may appear as a distinct and separate layer on top of the clay. The distinction can be capitalized on in many ways. Glazes can be seen as independent from the clay. The expression can be frankly involved with glass, with color, with reflection, with lusters and iridescences, with depths and layers of color, and with graphic articulations of line, area, texture, or brushwork. As an example, Persian tiles and plates owe little to clay; their beauty is in the glaze.

Glaze can enhance form. Enhancement occurs just in the tactile feel of glaze as compared to clay—smoothness, coolness, a jadelike feel under the fingers. The run or drape of glaze over a form can serve to define its contours in ways which do not depend on profile or shadow. Overlappings, cascading layers, pourings, or drippings can caress the form, stretching across, over, or around it, amplifying its swellings and turnings (Figure 171).

The multiplicity of glaze formulae and colors present difficult choices to the potter. Any color or texture is possible. How to choose, to narrow down the options to some workable selection? Most potters go through a diffuse period during which they try out numerous effects. Gradually, as their vision clarifies and as their uncertainty gives way to strongly held preferences, they begin to restrict their glazes to those which fit into an overall concept growing perhaps out of the form of the pots. It is said that Shoji Hamada, the great Japanese potter, uses only six glazes, yet no one would suggest that his work is lacking in variety. It is better to use a few glazes well than to indulge in a parade of colors and textures, none of which have much relationship to the pots on which they appear.

Salt glazing has the sometimes very beneficial effect of limiting the choice of glaze to one basic surface, a surface which can, however, be easily modified by slips or fuming to produce various colors. Salt glazing, since it is not applied but occurs as a vapor deposit, covers the pot more or less uniformly and thinly, and the "added on" look is minimized; the clay is still seen and felt through the glaze, which by its thinness and colorlessness, does not proclaim itself to be important or even admirable. It is serving the pot. The crystalline glaze is quite the opposite. In this case, the pot may be totally subordinate to the beauty and interest of the glaze.

The unifying, universal factor in the art of pottery is form. Glaze may clothe this form, enhance it, amplify it, define it, color it, waterproof it. But while pottery can and does exist without glazes, glazes are dependent upon the pot.

26 DECORATION

Pottery has been decorated in a great variety of techniques and different styles. In the past, the decoration on pottery was normally of a traditional sort; that is, the decoration followed closely the prevailing graphic styles and design motifs. Unlike pottery forms, which have by usage achieved a somewhat universal quality, the decorations on pots are more specifically related to particular cultures and eras.

It might be expected therefore, that the designs on pots today would echo or be related to the contemporary arts of painting and drawing and to some extent they are. But the fact is that contemporary styles in these arts are so personal, so various and changing that there is nothing resembling a tradition that can be drawn upon. The potter finds himself in the same position as any other artist; he must create out of his own personal vision a viable and communicable art. The difficulty of this path can hardly be overstated.

The best decorations on ceramics today seem to be done less in a spirit of "decorating" something and more as a form of communication at various levels about things which may involve fantasy, humor, satire, double entendre, or the macabre. Photo transfer and other novel processes are being used now which enlarge the decorator's vocabulary and make him less dependent on traditional techniques.

Decoration is not mandatory. The potter can allow or encourage decoration to come into his work only to the extent that it seems right. If there is no decoration at all, he still has the basic media of form to work with. Actually, a certain kind of decoration comes about just from the processes of forming. Throwing marks are natural to a wheel-made pot and may contribute an integrated surface pattern inseparable from the form and the action involved. Many analogies could be drawn from nature where the growth of stem, pod, or shell creates surface markings expressive of the actual development of the form. Similarly, the processes of trimming, manipulation of the clay by hand or tool, or the textures and surface variations which result from glazing and firing can result in modulated surfaces which belong intimately with the form. To the dictum "form follows function" could be added "surface results from the actions of process on the material."

Pottery Form

That such rules only point to one way of many is certainly proved by the history of pottery, which is replete with great examples where function is defied—if indeed there is even a reference to one—and where surface has been manipulated in ways which have nothing to do with pottery processes. There are no rules, only opportunities. The potter may start by relying only on those surface effects which come without much planning or forcing; with these he can work with freedom and self-confidence. Enrichment can come by stages. Even the most simple and uncomplicated pottery surface, a plain unglazed red earthenware, for example, has considerable interest and the forthright quality of a plain material not masquerading as anything else. Plain bare clay—brown, white, salmon, or black—has an earthy feel and look quite unlike any other material. The potter can always regard this clay quality as one of the basic aesthetic potentials of his craft. Whatever he does to a pot in the way of complicating or covering its surface with slips, glazes, and so forth, is not *necessary,* in the sense that painting a canvas is necessary if it is to be regarded as an art work. (It should be mentioned that the American artist Robert Rauchenberg exhibited a room-full of unpainted canvasses at the Parsons Gallery in New York, and that James Melchert once exhibited an unopened sack of dry clay.)

The history of pottery shows that the urge to decorate has been strong and constant since prehistoric times. The undecorated pot is more the exception than the rule. The Jomon pottery of prehistoric Japan, first made several thousands of years ago, has a highly developed decorative surface. This pottery seems to indicate that men living in an isolated culture with little to influence their craft except what they made themselves, will feel the need to decorate and enrich the surfaces of clay pots with lines and textures. The soft, freshly made pot presents a tempting surface on which the urge to draw, to measure, to divide, to define, to articulate, to enrich, to particularize, and to compose is projected. Far from being trivial or casual, the decoration on many primitive pots is a profoundly felt ordering of surface, often complex and subtle in relationships.

Pottery decoration has developed into what could almost be considered a separate art. It uses the graphic means of drawing and painting, employing lines, areas, textures, colors. These are spread out on a three-dimensional form and exist not as a picture but as an extension or modulator of space. Of course there are other art objects where graphic elements appear on form; for example, painted masks and sculptures in Africa, the decoration of tools and implements, and architecture. But the simplicity of pottery gives more scope for design than do the more complex forms of sculpture, tools, and buildings. The potter created a unity between surface and form, between colors, lines, and textures and the curving, continuous field of the pot's surface.

Historically, as pottery decoration became more pictorial and less abstract, it tended to lose its relationship with the pot. Whereas many "primitive" pots have decorations that cannot be conceived of apart from the pottery surface and form, European pottery (beginning with the Greeks and continuing through the traditions of the Italian Renaissance and to the later porcelains of France and Germany) increasingly used pottery as a field for pictorial art, a mere background or canvas for the display of virtuosity in painting. Thus the love affair between the pot and its decoration suffered rupture. In this process, the form of the pot became a thing of no great consequence. The seeds of this development were in Greek art, where noble pottery forms of ancient lineage came to be given standardized interpretations. Toward the fourth or fifth century B.C., the body, feet, and handles of Greek pots became stiff, controlled, and lifeless. The clay no longer *moved,* it merely served to hold up the painting. That marvelous attunement of design to form which the Greeks had achieved in the geometric period was lost. This is not to demean the achievements of the Greek vase painters, and their incredible ability to fill a space gracefully. It is just that the decoration achieved total dominance over the form.

As interest in the form of the pot declines and the decoration becomes dominant, the integral relationship between the two may suffer. The Persians of the Islamic period, who inherited and developed a great Turkoman tradition in decorative art, treated the pot primarily as a field for the working out of pattern and color. Their pieces are rich and glowing, even sumptuous in some cases. But form is de-emphasized. Most of the masterworks of Persian pottery are plates or low bowls, and their shapes, while often satisfactory, never achieve the cool perfection of the Chinese. The designs on the insides of bowls are perfectly adapted to the circular format. In upright pieces such as ewers and jars, we sense first the power of the decoration and are aware of the form as a lesser factor.

Conversely, during the Sung period in China (A.D. 960–1280), certainly one of the pinnacles of ceramic art, potters seemed primarily interested in form, and decoration was employed only minimally. Of course there was great concentration on glaze and on the achievement of certain colors, the glazes being usually monochromes without patterns or brushwork. The forms of the pots at their best hover around the interior; an aura of movement is felt within a timeless frame. Clay remains clay. Its fixation by fire enables us to follow the fingers of the potter as our own fingers trace his movement over the form. No imposed geometry or pictorialism could have amplified these pots. Later, in the Ming period (A.D. 1368–1644), the advent of blue decoration over white porcelain shifted interest away from form and more toward decoration. But a beautiful relationship between the two persisted for several centuries, with decoration developing great complexity and sophistication. At last, after about the middle of the eighteenth century, decadence set in and the pottery surface became primarily a field for painting.

Clay pots, being made of a soft impressionable material can be decorated by impressions in the clay itself. Scratching, stamping, incising, and paddling or beating can produce textures, lines, areas, or low relief. Sprigs can be fastened onto the surface to give a sculptured surface. All of these many ways of enriching the clay surface itself have the virtue of being an integral part of the substance of the pot rather than something painted on; it therefore has a more likely chance, perhaps, of seeming to belong.

One type of pottery surface which might be considered a kind of decoration is that change of color and texture which comes about through the action of the fire on the material. Such surface variations, since they are largely or altogether accidental, might not fit precisely the meaning of the term "decoration," since that implies conscious art. An analogy would be the grain of wood as it is seen on furniture or implements; it may enhance the appearance and intensify the meaning of the form, but it was not put there by the furniture maker. In a sense, he found it as he cut into his material. In like manner, the potter commits his pieces to the kiln, perhaps without glaze or decoration of any sort, and after firing finds that the fire and ash, the very atmosphere of the kiln, has conferred certain marks, flashings, glazed areas, streaks, granules or roughnesses. The pot, as it came to permanence in the fire has taken on an enriched surface without being touched by the potter. For the most part, potters have abjured such firing variations and have struggled to get the process under control to the extent that effects can be predicted and reproduced. Primitive potters early learned how to manage the fire to get plain red pots rather than black ones or partly red and partly black. The ancient Chinese, as their understanding and control over ceramic processes developed, were able to keep the accidental to a minimum and, judging by what remains, they destroyed many pieces which did not meet their standards of perfection.

In Korean and Japanese pottery, accident and the sometimes uncontrollable effects of the fire played an important role in pottery. During the Silla period in Korea (57 B.C.–A.D. 935), unglazed grey stoneware pots were made to be placed in tombs with the deceased. These pots were fired in open kilns unprotected by saggers or muffles, and they often received coatings of glaze from the ash carried through the kiln from the fire by the draft. These ash-glazed areas gave a richness and interest to the bare clay and often emphasized the incised designs. A similar and contemporary Japanese pottery, the Sue, was a prototype for some of the Japanese stonewares. Early Japanese stoneware pots, made at Bizen, Shigaraki, Seto, and Tamba were at first unglazed and undecorated. But they frequently bore spectacular glazings and colorations from the flame and ash which complicated their surfaces in unpredictable ways. The kilns of Bizen continued making unglazed pots for several centuries. An unplanned decoration has given these Bizen pots a special interest. The pots were packed in the kiln with straw, which left brownish streaks on the finished pot. The position, color, and frequency of these streaks were almost entirely accidental. Because of their interest in the natural and unassuming qualities of folk art, Japanese tea masters loved these pots, which became identified with quietism and spontaneity. They seem to have "just happened," to have been, as Bernard Leach says, born, not made. Self-glazed or kiln-streaked pottery is part of a tradition which values the casual, the crooked, and the "kiln accident." Kiln accidents, a sense of the vulnerability of the pot, can reinforce the intimate and rather tender touches which make Japanese pottery distinctive from that of any other culture.

Pottery decoration runs a gamut from the integral geometry of primitive cultures to the soft pictorialism of Miessen, from the unplanned markings on old Japanese water jars to the tightly controlled programming of a Greek vase. For the modern potter, decoration is of necessity a very personal matter. There is no living tradition to which he can attach himself. It is an uncharted sea of possibilities.

SLIP DECORATION

This book, dealing with pottery form, is not the place for a discussion of all methods of decoration. Actually, ceramic decorative process is a very large and complex subject, and to thoroughly describe all the various methods would require a sizable volume. Since slip decoration grows out of the clay of the pot, a summary of the methods involved and their import for form will perhaps be useful. (For a discussion of the composition of slips for various kinds of pottery bodies, slip colors, and suitable glazes for slips see the author's *Clay and Glazes for the Potter*.)

The use of colored slips on pottery predates the development of glaze. In pre-Columbian America, where the potters never developed glaze, the use of slips reached a high stage of refinement and complexity. Neolithic pottery from many areas is decorated with colored clay. The use of slips under glazes was practiced in many lands, and an almost endless variety of techniques and styles evolved. Slips came to be the basic vehicle for pottery decoration.

Overleaf, top left to bottom right.
Fig. 165   Slip trailing.
Fig. 166   Brushed slip. The order of brush strokes and the direction and energy of the brush are plainly evident.
Fig. 167   Slip decoration. Sgraffito lines are cut through the white slip into the darker clay below. In this example and in the other examples of slip decoration, I have used a free interpretation of the Chinese character chi, *meaning "earth."*
Fig. 168   Paper resist slip decoration.

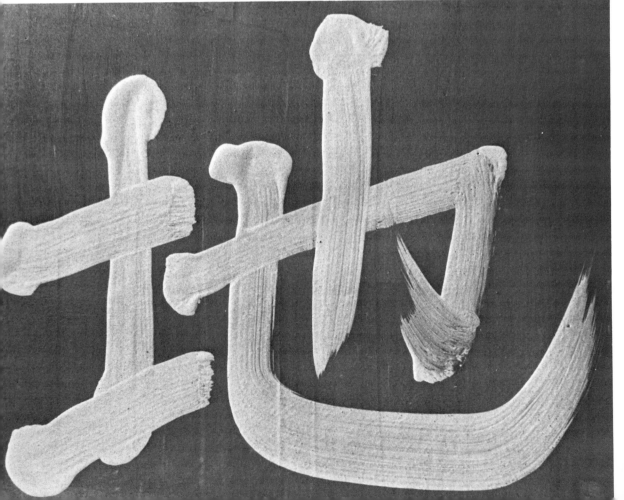

OVERALL SLIP COATINGS

Slip has often been used to change or to obscure the color of the clay body. Coatings of white or light colored slips were used in China to make dark stonewares appear lighter. In Europe, when the whiteness of Oriental porcelains was being sought after, potters coated their earthenwares with white slips to give them the prestige associated with the lighter tonalities.

The piece to be slipped should be on the dry side of leather hard. The slip can be brushed on, using a broad soft brush. Turning the pot on a banding wheel will make the brushings more uniform and even. Usually more than one coat is required, and the difficulty is to get the slip on evenly. Sometimes the first coat is colored with a vegetable dye (which burns off in the firing) then the next coat can be put on with a clear idea of what has already been covered. Thin places may show up under the glaze even though they are hard to detect in the raw state. Brushing seems to go better when the slip is rather thin.

Perhaps a better method than brushing is dipping and pouring. This is done very much in the manner of glaze application. The pot must be leather hard. If the inside and the outside are both to be coated by pouring or dipping, the inside should be done first and allowed to dry for an hour or more before the outside is done, otherwise the pot may be broken by becoming sogged with water from the slip. The unfired pot must be dipped rather rapidly into the slip, and the water content of the slip and the dryness or wetness of the pot must be carefully adjusted to prevent breakage. Also, the pot, being raw, must be very carefully handled. Dipping or pouring gives a very even coating of slip and is much quicker than painting.

Finger combing is a type of decoration used very successfully by the Koreans. Immediately after the pot has been dipped in slip and while the surface is still soft and wet, the potter rakes his finger tips through the slip. This creates a wavy pattern of marks where the body shows through the thin places. Coarse wooden combs, or coarse broom-like brushes can also be used to comb into the wet slip.

SGRAFFITO

This beautiful technique was widely used by the Chinese and the Persians and by European and American folk potters. After the slip has been applied to the whole piece as described above, or applied in an area, it is cut into with a pointed tool, giving a linear pattern or design. The sgraffito design is usually done while the pot is still in the leather hard state, but it can be done later when the piece is dry. If the pot and the slip are still damp and soft, the scratching of the lines proceeds more smoothly. The tool needs only to dig through the slip to create a line on the white surface. Different tools of various widths and points will give a variety of lines, or parallel lines can be made with several points fastened together. The quality of sgraffito lines in slip is unique. The yielding surface (damp clay and slip) make the tool glide along with the ease of a gesture. Turnings and stoppings produce variations in the line, a kind of calligraphy. Very precise designs can be done in sgraffito as well as more free, loose, arm-swinging line patterns. When the sgraffito lines become dense and close together, the body color can begin to dominate.

BRUSHED SLIP

As noted above, the brush can be used to lay a coating of slip over an entire piece or over an area (Figure 166). It can also be used to apply the slip in separate and identifiable brush strokes. A little experimentation will show that various kinds of brushes produce distinctive brush strokes. The size of the brush, the shape given to the hairs, and the coarseness or fineness of the hairs all influence the character of the brush stroke.

The soft pointed brushes used by the Chinese and Japanese for calligraphy produce a brush stroke which is teardrop in shape, blunt on one end and coming to a sharp point. By varying the pressure when painting, the stroke can be made to have strong bloblike accents at the beginning and end. The brush is very versatile, as is proved by the range of brush stroke shapes in Chinese painting and calligraphy. The fact that the brush makes a stroke which perfectly suggests a bamboo leaf makes one wonder if it was not developed just for this purpose.

All brushes, even soft ones like the calligraphy brush, drag the slip somewhat and produce thick and thin places in the stroke. Under a glaze these thin places show up, even though they may not be apparent in the raw state. The thick and thin of the brush stroke, and the striations created by the brush hairs, indicate the pressures and the direction used by the painter. These indications tell of the dynamic forces which animate the brush, its "body work." Rather than holding the brush in the fingers like a pencil, Chinese and Japanese painters hold the brush in the fist with the hairs pointing straight down. This manner of holding the brush favors the involvement of the whole arm in the brush stroke.

In slip painting, the quality of the brush stroke, its "brushiness," will be lost if it is gone over or touched up. It has to be put down boldly, once and for all, for better or for worse. For this reason, slip painting with the brush does not become convincing until the painter has gained confidence, relaxation, and zest. Good results will not come from making just one or two examples. It is necessary to practice, to develop a method of approach, and to learn to let go. Among Westerners, the brush is not an everyday instrument of writing or drawing and to master it requires much practice.

Coarser brushes give more striations in the pull of the brush stroke and

213

make refinement of outline impossible. Any type of brush can be put to good use. The old-fashioned shaving brush gives a wonderful fat brush stroke. A small dime-store paint brush is good for squarish brush strokes. The Japanese make a coarse brush by pounding the end of a bamboo stick until it is a mass of fiber. These brushes give scraggly strokes, full of character. Brushes made from broomstraws were used by the Koreans to produce the *hakeme* style of slip decoration. The slip was quickly brushed onto the inside of bowls with a loaded brush, giving a swirling effect full of energy and direction. The coarseness of the broomstraws gave prominent texture to the slip.

SLIP TRAILING

In slip trailing, the slip is squeezed or allowed to flow from a small container through a nozzle; this results in a line (Figure 165). Slip trailing seems to have been invented by the English potters of the early seventeenth century. It was not used in ancient China or in Japan, but Japanese folk potters, especially at Tamba and Onda, were using trailed designs, perhaps influenced by European pottery, around the middle of the nineteenth century.

The traditional slip trailer is a small clay vessel which fits into the hand. The nozzle is made of a goose or turkey quill. Slip flows from the trailer by gravity; the flow being regulated by a small thumbhole which, when covered, stops the flow or, when open, permits it. A slip trailer can be fitted with two or more quills in tandem to make parallel lines. Or, if compartmentalized, the trailer can make lines of two or more colors.

A rubber syringe will work quite well, but it will have to be squeezed to produce the line of slip.

The fat uniform line produced by the trailer makes it somewhat akin to a cake decorator. The line naturally has a liquid flow and easily makes curving wormlike lines. But it can be used for more geometrical designs as well. The use of the slip trailer requires a lot of control, and the beginner will have trouble producing continuous and sure lines. It is very important to have the slip free from lumps so that it will flow freely through the nozzle.

The model for slip trailing will probably always be the work of Thomas Toft, whose elaborately decorated plates were made in England during the seventeenth century. Toft built up complex patterns using impasto lines—thick—often crosshatched. It is a wonder that these trailed lines did not crack off during drying or firing.

Slip trailing has the visual effect of an addition to the surface, a kind of low relief. Actually if a pot is trailed over with some of the same clay it is made of, thus producing welts, these trailed lines can appear prominently under certain glazes which tend to run off high places and puddle in low places. The low relief quality of slip trailed lines brings them into a close relationship with the substance of the pot.

214

RESISTS

Various resist techniques are possible with slips (Figure 168). Wax can be painted or dipped on the pot, covering those areas which are not to receive slip. The slip is then poured or dipped onto the pot, rolling off the waxed portions. The wax burns off in the bisque fire. Or the wax may be painted on the leather hard pot in patterns, areas, lines, or any configuration desired, giving a resist to the slip.

Paper resist is another slip technique. The desired pattern or area is cut from a piece of newspaper. This is dampened and attached to the pot or tile with water. The slip is then poured or dipped on. The slip adheres to both paper and clay, but after a short period of drying the paper can be lifted off, showing the bare clay underneath.

The use of resists in slip introduces the possibility of positive-negative effects. Several layers of different colored slips can be laid on over one another, and resist areas blocked out in each one in turn. Or pour and splash effects can be done in wax to be defined by the surrounding slip.

INLAY

The inlay technique seems to have been an invention of Korean potters of the Koryu period. The technique was not used in China and did not appear in Japan until after the migration of Korean potters to that country during the late sixteenth century.

The design is scratched or incised into the damp clay with a sharp tool. The incised lines need not be deep. Then slip is painted over the incised lines and worked thoroughly into it. After the slip has dried somewhat, the excess slip is scraped away from the surface, leaving only that which has collected in the scratches. The effect is that of an inlayed line of clay of a different color than the body of the pot. Several colors can be inlaid in turn. Korean inlay pots of the Koryu dynasty (A.D. 918–1392) were done with much precision and carefully worked out detail. Pots made later in Korea during the Yi Dynasty (A.D. 1392–1910) were inlaid in a more loose style. All of the excess slip was not scraped away, which made the lines slightly blurred in places. Stamps rather than hand-incised lines were sometimes used to impress the clay for the inlay.

The inlay technique is rather slow and painstaking, but it can be effective for making precise, controlled lines or to create patterns. Its slowness practically rules it out for the potter who must make the most of his time.

SLIP COMBING

This is a rather specialized technique which was used in England and to some extent in colonial American folk pottery. It takes advantage of the wet, flowing quality of slip (Figure 164). First, the clay is covered with stripes or bands of slips of different colors. For instance, black slip bands might be alternated with white or grey bands. These bands are applied in such a way that the slip of each band is laid so as to touch the slip of the next band, with no bare clay showing in between. Laying in these bands of slip is best done by holding the clay slab in a tilted position and then applying the slip with a large syringe, letting it flow downward over the clay. After the desired number of bands are laid in, a pin point or the end of a feather is drawn through the wet slip in a direction opposite to the bands. The point drags the slip from one band into the next in pointed configurations. The point's direction of travel can be alternated to cause the resulting configurations to go in the opposite direction, or the strokes of the point can be grouped in twos or threes, with space in between. Many variations are possible depending on how the bands are laid down in the first place and how the combings are done. The effect is apt to be one of intricate and rather mysteriously controlled detail.

Combing must be carried out on damp clay, because if the clay is too dry the bands of slip will settle in and become too stiff before the combing can be finished. For plates and low bowls, the combing is usually done on a flat slab of clay, and when the combing has set up a bit, the clay is picked up and forced down over a plaster or bisque clay mold, decorated side down. This molding process has the effect of flattening any low relief in the slip, causing it to look almost like an inlay in the finished, glazed piece. When molding a plate, a piece of clay larger than the actual area of the mold is used; after the clay has been laid over the mold, it is trimmed off around the edge, much as one trims a pie crust around the pie tin.

The limitation of slip combing is that it always looks more or less alike no matter who does it, and the interest in the resulting pattern is more one of curiosity than aesthetic appreciation. It is somewhat mechanical, rather the opposite of brush work.

SLIP JOLTING

A variation on slip combing is slip jolting. In this technique, the slab from which the plate is to be made is put on the wheel. Slip is poured onto it in a willy-nilly fashion—two or more colors being put on in globs or bands. Then the wheel is quickly turned, causing the wet slip to fly away from center. The various areas blend unpredictably. It is a chance design. Pennsylvania Dutch potters made plates this way.

COMBINING TECHNIQUES

Several slip application techniques can be combined effectively. For example, wax resist can be used to define certain areas of slip and then sgraffito or trailing can be added for linear pattern.

Fig. 169 Opposite. *Footed ovoid jar. The pattern is light slip inlaid in the brown clay.*

27 APPROACHES TO STUDY

A study of pottery-making usually takes the form of extended practice, during which skills are gradually developed and the emerging forms made more and more in keeping with the practical and aesthetic dimensions of the craft as the potter sees them. Since the student's view of the various aspects of the craft will always be changing, especially while he is actively working, study will not have an end but will extend to conform to his working career.

An important part of learning pottery is the development of maximum feedback from, and awareness of the objects being made. Many work at pottery for years without ever really seeing, feeling, or experiencing their own work except in the most cursory way. There are some practical ways to increase intimacy with one's own work.

Seeing one's pot on the wheel as it develops is aided by the placement of a mirror at the wheel opposite the seat. With the aid of the mirror, the profile of the pot can be more clearly seen. Usually the potter sees his work somewhat from above. This tends to give an exaggerated impression of height relative to breadth, and a pot which is actually rather squatty will appear (perhaps partly by wishful thinking) to be higher and narrower than it actually is. When a pot on the wheel is nearing completion, it can be better studied by getting off the wheel and stepping aside a bit. From this view, many features of the pot will be more clearly seen than they were from the seated position. Many unsatisfactory pots result simply from having been declared finished before the potter has given himself the chance to sense, to see the work and to be alert to its as yet unrealized potentials.

The bone-dry piece can also be studied profitably. It is often very revealing to make an accurate full-scale drawing of a piece on paper, sketching in its exact profile. This drawn profile may reveal certain things about the shape and proportion which were only vaguely felt in the actual pot. A heaviness and slumping quality may be discovered which was only vaguely sensed before.

Cutting pieces in half while they are still soft reveals the actual cross section. This can obviously be done only to pieces which are already declared "just for practice." The thickness of a thrown piece can also be determined by pressing a pin through the wall until it just emerges on the other side. Such test holes fill with glaze, causing no later difficulties.

To study a dry, bisqued, or glazed piece, an isolated environment helps in bringing its features into clarity and focus. Ordinarily, when we look at pots in the usually crowded confusion of the pottery shop, it is difficult to really see one piece as an entity—its presence is confused by a multiplicity of visual signals and interferences. A study box or display box can easily be made from cardboard or an old crate, lit from the top with a light bulb shining through a hole. In such a box, painted white inside, the pot is placed for study. It will then appear as an isolated object, receiving neither positive nor negative vibrations from the outside. Pots seen in such a simplified surrounding will clearly reveal themselves, with all of their faults and virtues.

Photography performs somewhat the same function as the isolation box. In a photograph, the pot appears as an object separated physically from every other object and reduced to an image, a two-dimensional replica. Granted there is missing in the photograph a great deal of what can be known of a pot such as color, scale, weight, feel, tactile qualities, and the like. But sometimes a photograph, just *because* some of these other attributes are subtracted, will reveal to the potter certain truths about his work, pleasant or unpleasant. Students of dimensional art find the camera, with its controlled viewpoint and lighting, a useful tool for putting their own work into a new perspective.

Vision is only one of the senses involved in the encounter with pots. Touch is perhaps just as important, and this sense also is frequently neglected. Blind persons have learned to make quite satisfactory pots, and their knowledge of pots through feeling can be extensive. In wheel work, as mentioned earlier, just slowing down the wheel will bring a sensation of closer tactile relationship with the spinning clay. From time to time the thrower should forget what he sees and try to be more aware of what is felt in the hands. More spontaneous work can result from the relaxation of vision with its built-in evaluating habits. It is sometimes forgotten that the cross section of a pot on the wheel can be quite accurately sensed through the fingers, and that the ins and outs of a form as determined by the fingers

Fig. 170 Overleaf left. *Pitcher (shown unfired in Figure 78). Firing has given the piece an overall texture. The upper rim, the ridge marking the bottom of the collar, and the form of the handle have been accentuated by the glaze. At the bottom, unglazed clay contrasts with the glaze.*
Fig. 171 Overleaf right. *Glazed bottle (shown unfired in Figure 37). The flow of glaze downward defines the form and breaks its symmetry.*

themselves may have a more natural, a more relaxed character than form which is first visualized, then made to order by the hands.

Another exercise is to set aside, instead of collapsing, freshly made pots which are felt to be unsatisfactory for one reason or another. When these have stiffened up a bit they are further worked by the hands alone. Thick places can be thinned by the pressure of the fingers. Forms can be made to bulge or to cave in, and rims can be varied by thinning or bending. In this way, the form, born but not matured on the wheel, can grow and change, and the potter can become directly aware of the weight, the feel, and the shape of his work.

One-handed throwing is sometimes done as a stunt, and it is a fact that a good thrower can make small pieces quite easily with one hand only. The fact that the left hand is almost always used for this points to its equal, if not predominate role in throwing. Throwing with one hand does give a different tactile experience, and for beginners it can help to give an idea of the pressures required in throwing. To squeeze the revolving clay between the thumb and forefinger until it gives and thins sometimes awakens a sensory response in the fingers; a knowledge of what makes the clay move. One-handed throwing can be practiced with the blindfold or in a darkened room to eliminate, for a time, the factor of visual ordering.

One of the distinctions of pottery is that our normal encounters with it involve touch as well as sight. Pottery in use is handled, picked up, lidded and unlidded, and brought to the mouth. In former times it was the primary food container and cooking vessel, the bathtub, toilet, and even the casket. Sculpture also is a highly tactile art, but it is felt only as a directed aesthetic experience whereas we encounter pottery in many ways. Its form, texture, and weight exert a subliminal influence on our senses. The best way to study one's pottery is to use it. It will then be realized that some of the qualities of a pot are not immediately obvious and become more apparent with time and use. This works both ways. Some pieces which seem right when they are taken from the kiln will lose some of their appeal after being used for a time and vice versa. Functional shortcomings which at first were thought to be more than counterbalanced by "charm" may become unacceptable.

Most artists and craftsmen receive both positive and negative vibrations from their work, an on-off, yes-no signal which varies with mood, amount of time elapsed since finishing the work, and comparisons made inevitable by the creation of later examples. Negative criticisms, justified or not, may come from relatives, friends, or critics. The negative impressions should be neither suppressed nor allowed to dominate or inhibit later work. To be able to face up to the shortcomings of one's own work and go on from there is an indispensable part of learning. But if the spirit is to find expression in the work, a certain tenderness towards it and toward the medium must be manifest. Just to make a pot is an act of affirmation—an object is brought into reality where, hopefully, it will find some place and function, however marginal. Self-doubt and self-criticism beyond a certain point are destructive and inhibiting, and one of the lessons which must be learned is to forgive ourselves for less than perfect, less than inspiring work.

A change in the actual pace of working can sometimes be helpful. A spell of working much faster than usual can bring about a loosening of form, and a lessening of attention to the niceties of detail and finish. It is a good exercise for those who have a tendency toward tightness of form or the tendency to "design" rather than "make" their pots. There is no doubt that some of the qualities which we admire in certain old pots can be accounted for in part by the brisk pace at which they were made, with the attendant lack of concern for petty detail or fine finish. Old Korean rice bowls come to mind as an example. They seem to have opened up on the wheel as naturally as a morning glory blossom.

On the other hand, drastically slowing down the pace of the work can bring another kind of opportunity for growth. Working on the wheel, especially seems to bring on a somewhat fixed pattern of rapid accomplishment. Legendary throwers, who can produce a hundred cups an hour are emulated. Of course there is nothing wrong with speedy potting. But for relief and variety, other approaches could alternate with rapid throwing. Hand building, coiling, and modeling by their nature require much time, and in the slow emergence of form a different kind of communion with the clay occurs. One need not always approach the clay as if a time/motion study were being made; times arise which can be set aside for a more meditative experience.

Pottery-making can be *karma yoga,* or centeredness through action. The turning wheel, the rhythms of throwing with its steady flow of energy from hand to clay, the gestures of wedging, glazing, decorating, and the transmutations of the fire—all of these involve selfless concentration, the letting go of everything except the work at hand.

Creative work never seems to proceed in a straight line. There are false starts, errors, lapses, sudden bursts of progress or insight, failures, periods of frustration and discouragement, and, hopefully, periods of steady

Fig. 172 Overleaf left. *Covered jar (shown unfired in Figure 99). Glaze has given highlights to the throwing marks, making them more noticeable. Enriched texture toward the upper part of the piece gives emphasis to the rise of form from base to lid, and suggests the effect of the fire. The spiral on the top of the lid is made prominent by the pooling of glaze.*
Fig. 173 Overleaf right. *Thrown and slab-built pot (shown unfired in Figure 122). The glaze has given a rich overall texture and has emphasized the throwing marks, joints, incised lines and ridges.*

progress. Pottery-making, since it usually involves some repetitious work has a relatively steady quality about it. But even so, it has its inevitable ups and downs. The downs should be considered part of the experience; failures can be used to expand, deepen, and enrich the work.

For one reason or another, a percentage of pots do fail to actualize. They are too thick, or too thin, they become crooked or warped, they break or crack, they are damaged by falling or accident, or, more frequently, their form ends up so far from the potter's ideal that the pot is declared a dud. One of the good things about pottery-making is that these failures can be tossed back in the soaking pit and the clay reclaimed for use in another pot.

However, before consigning a piece to the scrap, it can be used as a study in metamorphosis, a rebirth to another form. Working on a piece which has already been declared a failure brings about a relaxation of one's feelings toward that piece which is the very condition often lacking when we are trying to work at peak capacity and creativity. If you don't care what happens to a piece, you may be willing to try things you would not try ordinarily. So the discarded pot can be cut, bent, added to, subtracted from, resoftened and reshaped, punched with holes or openings, textured, beaten, or stamped. Perhaps it can be combined with other discards to make a wholly new form. For example, a group of, say, six "no good" mugs could be used as cylinders to build a tall cylindrical pot.

Granted, the results of such experiments on discarded pieces may not result in work which is worthy of the fire. But the experience of relaxed playfulness with form can lead to enlarged concepts about the work as a whole. Thus the effort put into the piece in the first place, becomes part of the whole process of one's encounter with the clay rather than being wasted.

Pots which are felt to be unfit for the fire are a perfect field for practicing decoration of various kinds. Here again, relaxation is possible because there is nothing to lose, and to decorate a pot "just for fun" re-creates in a way the mood which must have prevailed during most of pottery history when the decorators worked on pots which they did not make. If a mistake was made, there was always another pot on the rack and not much was lost. All manner of surface variations, can be tried on discarded pots and out of such half-serious trys hints may come of possibilities not envisioned before.

Most ceramic accidents are the result of the vagaries of firing, but some unfired pots do become the victims of bumps, falls, wettings, freezings, and the like. Rather than declaring such injured pots a total loss, they can be nursed along a little and made to play out their role to the end. The end will probably be the scrap bucket, but before that finality the piece may yield valuable insights, hints of perhaps radical new solutions to problems.

Negative impulses are normal. They are the dark side, the obverse side

is obvious; and in shaping the pot, empathy for its form and for its dark cavity must have been felt. The pot has a strong analogy with the feminine principle. Its function is to hold, to preserve, to protect, to receive, and to give out. The pot is centered about its cavity. Projections, yes, in the form of handles, spouts, or knobs, but the thrust of form is inward, always coming back to center.

What is implicit in the storage jar becomes explicit in the effigy pot. These were made in many cultures from very ancient times. Whole human figures as pots, heads as pots, animals as pots. Human mouths became the entrance of the pot. Penises became spouts. Arms became handles. These effigy pots are actually a special kind of sculpture in which the form is developed as a sculptural concept, an image, yet the integrity of the interior, the hollow is carefully preserved. It cannot be doubted that in making and using these effigies man gained self-knowledge and self-awareness.

It is this universal image, built into the family of pottery forms, and signifying life, generation, protection, and survival, which gives to certain pots an aura, a mystical presence. Perhaps this quality is largely missing from pots made today. I am thinking more of pots made in societies where the potter worked in harmony with his culture rather than as commentator, gadfly, or oddball, as it is with us in the twentieth century. This presence, when it is felt, makes the pot more than a pot. The space around the form seems energized. The center, the core of the pot is the focus of the forces put in motion by the dynamics of form and decoration. A subtle unity of form, function, surface, and substance transcends the separate parts. The pot is sensed through the eyes, through the fingers, through the muscles of hands and arms, through the mind; it is a completely realized expression. The pot—unlike many sculptures and paintings which demand or assume fixed locations on buildings or on pedestals—exists free in its environment, movable in response to the demands of its function.

In the Sung period in China, (A.D. 960–1279), perhaps the greatest period in the history of pottery, pots became established as forms in themselves, still carrying the functional imperative but released from slavery to it. The vase, the jar, the bottle, the bowl—these elemental shapes were perfected, refined by countless redefinitions. The forms approached the ultimate, a state totally beyond the realm of fancy, whimsy, or eccentricity. Pottery achieved the coolness, perhaps some of the remoteness of distant mountain peaks or islands in a lake. The potters seemed motivated by some larger purpose than their own, and their statements approached the universal. The image is one of finality, immutability, perfection, quiet, in-

Fig. 175 Overleaf. *Jar (shown unfired in Figure 16). Firing has imparted a variety of textures reminiscent of earthy material.*

231

wardness, timelessness. Celadon is moonlight, the black glazes of Honan are the dense midnight. The blue of Chun is the sky.

A potent image is projected from certain Japanese pots of the sixteenth and seventeenth centuries. I am thinking of pottery from Bizen, Tamba, Shigaraki, and Iga. These pieces relate to nature in its more specific, close-up phases. The image is one of rocks, minerals, vulcanism, flow of lava, roughness of bark or hide, water over granite rock, staining of iron, beach sands, rocky outcrops, patina of rocks in canyons, moss clinging to rock. Each piece seems a sudden emergence of something which will not recur. The fire is felt.

When my mind wanders over the various kinds of pottery from the past that have been meaningful to me, I am transported to the incredibly various and complex cultures of man. Through the pots I seem to feel the life that lies behind them. Especially vivid are the jars made by the Pueblo Indians in the prehistoric period and also in the eighteenth and nineteenth centuries. The decoration consists of graphic symbols which were known to all and which also appeared on textiles and in sand paintings. But the potters used them with a certain freedom and variation, combining, re-stating and welding together the signs for "rain," "mountain," and the like. The pot is inhabited by designs which spread out evenly over the surface, moving but not strongly directional. The patterns and the forms of the pots themselves suggest the Southwestern terrain. We seem to feel the clarified structure of the land, the clouds moving in concord with the shapes of the earth, and the ever changing light playing over mesas, mountains, and canyons. The pot—complete, centered, integrated, and serene—is a harmonious place where differentiation does not contradict unity. Parts interact, yet remain harmonious. The dynamics of form, line, and pattern achieve stasis in the whole. The image is one of a completed system, an ecology of nature. To create such pots, men had to be fundamentally at peace with their world, reacting to nature and to life with reverence.

(The Hopi woman was buried with some of the pots which she had made.)

29 POTTERY & THE PERSON

Most discussions of pottery, or historical references to it, give it a kind of impersonal existence, as if pots sprang into being as a result of process, almost without the intervention of people. Pots of the past are described in detail, but their makers are seldom mentioned. This is partly because the pottery of the past was largely an anonymous art, and nothing much specifically is known of the actual potters.

As we learn to make pots, and as we deal with the sometimes difficult and intricate facets of the craft, our attention is directed to the *pot,* to the thing we are making. The fact that the pot is but a reflection of our inner being, of where we are at the time, is not intruding into our consciousness, and this is well, because any art or any craft requires full, directed attention, and self-consciousness, while it may be revealing or even fruitful, has no place in the moment of expressive action.

Looked at subjectively, however, pottery-making can be thought of not so much as an activity resulting in so many bowls, cups, or jars of some assumed function, value, or aesthetic merit but rather as the outcome of our urge to form and, in forming the clay, to find our own form. The changes and developments in the form of the clay which passes through our fingers can parallel, complement, signify, and support the changes and the evolution of our own inner consciousness. To form is to actualize, to bring into reality what was not there before, to create one's image, to expand and to develop this image. This impulse to form is basic to the human condition, existing among all of the tribes.

Today, the impulse to form, and the opportunity to deal directly with our own self as projected in tangible form in the outer sphere, is thwarted. Mechanization, industrialization, division of labor, commercialism, and standardization have wiped out most of the formerly abundant opportunities for the individual to function through craft. Great gains bring great

Fig. 176 Opposite. *Slab-built pot (shown unfired in Figure 162). The flow and pooling of the glaze clothes the form.*

losses, and men and women have been left with a feeling of being cut off from themselves with a loss of identity.

Craft, almost eliminated from the practical world and a seeming anachronism, has become a precious remnant. In it, we can sense the potential for full development of the person, for the restoration of wholeness. The artist and the craftsman, laboring outside of society's system of production-money-consumption, keep alive a different way of working and living. They work for the joy of working and they seek and find their identity in the work of their own hands rather than in commercialized images on screen or paper, images projected by promoters of a world which does not exist.

The way of the artist and the craftsman is difficult. Cut off from the main thrust of his society, he must go it alone. The very traditions from which he seeks nourishment tend to wither, to become weakened and confused. There is the problem of finding bread. The artist working within the context of fine arts as they are defined in our culture, faces almost insuperable difficulties. He is cut off from any coherent tradition which might be shared with others in a supportive way. Alone, he struggles to assert his original and personal statement. By definition, his statement, since it must be starkly original and not based on the past, will be illegible except perhaps to a few. Obsolescence and neglect follow directly on success, a success which in any case is improbable in the extreme. The life of the dedicated artist can only be regarded as a heroic encounter, a struggle against impossible odds. It is significant that the work of children, folk artists, or the naive often has a freshness, vitality and charm lacking in "professional" art; these less sophisticated artists are still able to work without undue self-consciousness or concern about the ultimate meaning or acceptability of their work.

The potter works toward more modest goals than the sculptor or painter. He creates something of utility; aesthetic values are not its sole justification. With intelligence, skill, and practice he is reasonably assured of making something of value. Pottery exists within a framework or boundary—perhaps defined as constricting by some—but within this defined area some measure of security can be found. For the craftsman, function is a balance wheel. It is something to work with (or, in searching for the boundaries of one's expression, to work against). It is a fixed point of reference. To the question, "For whom is this work?" the "fine" artist can answer only that he hopes his work will eventually find an audience and move them as he has been moved. The potter can answer; "I present this pot, which embodies my skill, my insight, my respect for the material and process, my sincere search for form. It will be useful in the kitchen and on the table. It may bring a small touch of warmth and beauty to those who use it. Whatever exists in it which might be called 'art' will function through daily use, through touch, through intimate acquaintance."

Pottery-making then, is a shaping of material, a postulation of form, an actualization of dreams which can occur in a natural way without an undue challenge to the ego. It is not pretentious. Its commitments have to do with right making more than with exhibitionism. The potter can achieve a certain relaxation in his work, learn to be comfortable with it. Out of this natural relationship to work may grow a natural expression of self, an unforced, unselfconscious, genuine flow of person to pot. However modest, the pot can be an authentic image of the potter.

To find reality in one's work, to project honestly into it, is to become *centered*. For better or worse, the pot becomes the projection of the potter, his image. In it are summed up the integration of his powers, his thoughts, his feelings, his action. Pottery form is an emblem of this integration, and we must avoid thinking about the form of pots as if it were something impersonal. Forms grow from the person. That is why it is impossible to assign any hierarchy of value to pots or to impose standards aside from the equation *person = pots.*

I have talked about the various pottery forms in terms of their adaptations to various functions and how they were shaped. But the true import of forms, their vitality, cannot be analyzed because they are the outcome of complex generative forces at the point where the potter interacts with material and process.

As the development of personality is a slow process and a response to innumerable influences both external and internal, so the development of style in the work unfolds gradually. We are not making today what we made a year ago, and tomorrow we will be making something different, something not now imagined. The image grows, changes, fades or blurs at times, then sharpens, enlarges, becomes perhaps diffuse and then concentrated. These developments, like the changes in life, can bring joy, satisfaction, pain, or despair, but they must be lived. The evolution of the clay under the hands cannot be forced. Time is required for each stage. Each fallow period must be endured; the seemingly negative factors in the work, after the passage of time and more work, may turn out to be faltering steps in the right direction. Failures can be defined as searches in the byways, and as such can be absorbed without damage to the self.

Pottery requires on one hand active effort, concentration, and tension, and on the other, relaxation. These two qualities, in fact, can be identified in many pots. Some pots, such as certain ones made in classical Greece or Etruria, are tense, sharply fashioned, with exaggerated curves and relationships between parts. Handles rise from the rims with sprightly vigor, and feet are made almost as separate forms. Some old Chinese pots are almost

limp by comparison. Their proportions are modest, their parts closely integrated. The clay has not been asked to do that which is difficult for it. Of these two qualities, relaxation is the hardest for us to achieve. That is why the works of the contemporary Japanese potter Shoji Hamada are so impressive. Each of his pots, although usually modest in scale and in proportion, speaks of a sense of ease. The clay has not been pushed beyond a certain point. They are in the tradition of Zen inspired arts—"No Fuss."

Pottery as meditation, as selfless concentration, requires the abandonment of anxiety and the perfection of skill to the point where it can be forgotten and one's consciousness becomes absorbed in the tactile sensations of process. In this state, the work will form itself, and the potter may feel presumptuous even to take credit for the happenings which emerge from his kiln. The question of originality will have been solved. Who asks whether their own pattern of speech and expression are original? No one, because we all achieve originality in speech by a lifetime of concentration on what is said rather than how it is said.

As in the growth of plants, the emergence of forms from the hands proceeds in small steps, gradual unfoldings. One must be satisfied with small gains, evolution rather than sudden revelation.

The potter approaches the clay with just his hands. There is no intervening superstructure, no frozen or mechanized system, no network of authority between him and his work. The forms he makes are his alone.

Fig. 177 Opposite. *Compression pot (shown unfired in Figure 160). The progression of textures creates an upward movement. Encrustations at the bottom bring to mind moss on rock.*

239

INDEX

Index

DANIEL RHODES is a potter, sculptor, author, and teacher. His work in clay, and his teaching and writing, have had a significant influence in the world of ceramics. A native of Iowa, he began his artistic career as a painter, meeting early success as a muralist and draftsman. Turning to clay he began an intensive exploration of ceramics which has resulted in a large body of work. In the 1950s he participated in the upsurge of ceramic art; since then his work has been a feature of many important exhibitions. He has had numerous one-man shows of sculpture, pottery, and graphics, the first of which was held at the California Palace of the Legion of Honor in 1948. Rhodes received a Fulbright research grant in 1962 for a year of study in Japan.

Prior to 1973 he was professor of art at Alfred University, and many of his former students are in the first rank of American ceramists. His contributions to ceramic literature include four books in addition to the present volume, and many articles and papers. His first book, *Clay and Glazes for the Potter,* is known as "the potter's Bible." *Stoneware and Porcelain* and *Kilns* have also become standard reference works. *Tamba Pottery* resulted from his study in Japan. At present he lives in California on the Santa Cruz North Coast.